D0208743

"If your teens are asking about God and life, Gwendolyn Mitchell Diaz gives superb, innovative answers to 'why believe' questions. She knows teens, and explains her answers with excellent illustrations and applications from their own world. I want to read this book again!"

— *Marie H. Little, Mrs. Paul E. Little;*
author, updated six of Paul E. Little's books

STICKING UP FOR WHAT I BELIEVE

ANSWERS TO THE SPIRITUAL QUESTIONS TEENAGERS ASK

Gwendolyn Mitchell Diaz

NAVPRESS

BRINGING TRUTH TO LIFE

P.O. Box 35001, Colorado Springs, Colorado 80935

YEARY LIBRARY
LAREDO COMM. COLLEGE
LAREDO, TEXAS

OUR GUARANTEE TO YOU

We believe so strongly in the message of our books that we are making this quality guarantee to you. If for any reason you are disappointed with the content of this book, return the title page to us with your name and address and we will refund to you the list price of the book. To help us serve you better, please briefly describe why you were disappointed. Mail your refund request to: NavPress, P.O. Box 35002, Colorado Springs, CO 80935.

The Navigators is an international Christian organization. Our mission is to reach, disciple, and equip people to know Christ and to make Him known through successive generations. We envision multitudes of diverse people in the United States and every other nation who have a passionate love for Christ, live a lifestyle of sharing Christ's love, and multiply spiritual laborers among those without Christ.

NavPress is the publishing ministry of The Navigators. NavPress publications help believers learn biblical truth and apply what they learn to their lives and ministries. Our mission is to stimulate spiritual formation among our readers.

© 2002 by Gwendolyn Diaz

All rights reserved. No part of this publication may be reproduced in any form without written permission from NavPress, P.O. Box 35001, Colorado Springs, CO 80935. www.navpress.com

ISBN 1-57683-311-9
Cover design by Ray Moore
Cover illustration by Digital Vision 168074A
Creative Team: Paul Santhouse, Greg Clouse, Darla Hightower, Glynese Northam

Some of the anecdotal illustrations in this book are true to life and are included with the permission of the persons involved. All other illustrations are composites of real situations, and any resemblance to people living or dead is coincidental.

Unless otherwise identified, all Scripture quotations in this publication are taken from the HOLY BIBLE: NEW INTERNATIONAL VERSION® (NIV®). Copyright © 1973, 1978, 1984 by International Bible Society. Used by permission of Zondervan Publishing House. All rights reserved. Other versions include: the *New American Standard Bible* (NASB), © The Lockman Foundation 1960, 1962, 1963, 1968, 1971, 1972, 1973, 1975, 1977, 1995; and the *King James Version* (KJV).

Diaz, Gwendolyn Mitchell.
    Sticking up for what I believe : answers to the spiritual questions teenagers ask / Gwendolyn Mitchell Diaz.
        p. cm.
Includes bibliographical references.
    ISBN 1-57683-311-9
    1. Teenagers--Religious life--Miscellanea. I. Title.
    BV4531.3 .D53 2002
    239--dc21   2002002121

Printed in the United States of America
1 2 3 4 5 6 7 8 9 10 / 05 04 03 02

BV
4531.3
·D53
200

FOR A FREE CATALOG OF
NAVPRESS BOOKS & BIBLE STUDIES,
CALL 1-800-366-7788 (USA)
OR 1-416-499-4615 (CANADA)

JAN 1 6 2003

DEAR PARENT,

This book is based on discussions with my four sons: Zachary, Matthew, Benjamin, and Jonathan. I originally wrote it just for them, but they are allowing me to share it with you. Read it yourself to grasp better the spiritual questions your teens and preteens are asking; borrow the ideas and fill in your own stories to share at the appropriate moment; or loan it to your kids to read. What better place to dialogue honestly about the nitty-gritty issues of life than in the home.

GWENDOLYN MITCHELL DIAZ

CONTENTS

INTRODUCTION

Why Should I
Read This Book?

To answer your question, I need to take you to a cement school-yard in Ventnor, New Jersey, where I once played as a child. (Yes, believe it or not, your mom actually was a little girl a long time ago!) I was in the fourth grade at Ventnor Avenue Elementary School while my family was in the United States on furlough from their mission station in Nigeria, West Africa.

Up to that point my life had been relatively simple. I had spent the first five years growing up in the rugged isolation of a mission station. Since we were far removed from the normal progress of human history, life was basic and rough. We lived in a mud-brick house with no electricity or running water. That means no hot water heater, no hair dryer, no television set, no CD player! Instead of dogs and cats for pets, we had monkeys and deer. Instead of avoiding roaches and garden snakes, we were on the lookout for scorpions and cobras. Obviously we were forced to incorporate physical survival skills into the normal course of everyday life. Just making a peanut butter and jelly sandwich involved winnowing the wheat and picking the peanuts — for real!

However, those harsh years were softened by the loving tute-lage of my proud, inventive, American father (whom you know as "our Bupah who lives in heaven" since he passed away before any of you were born) and my well-spoken, genteel, English mother

(Granny, whom you know and love). As I look back, I recall bright, happy years full of adventure and learning.

Then I turned six, and life changed drastically. Suddenly I found myself deposited in the crowded chaos of a mission boarding school. Since the school was located in a more civilized part of Africa, physical survival skills were no longer essential. I took long hot showers and ate peanut butter and jelly sandwiches for snacks! However, the development of emotional survival skills became absolutely imperative. With so many children to care for, there wasn't enough parental love, guidance, or supervision to go around. These were definitely "growing up, discovering-one's-self" years filled with anxiety and pain, but I made it through.

All my life I had been taught to believe in and rely on God — a God who created all life, superseded all beings, and intervened throughout history; a God who was explained in the Bible. He was a vital component of my life at home and a rigid ingredient in my boarding school education.

If you wanted to, I guess you could sum up the first eight years of my life in a mathematical equation. It would look something like this:

$$5 \text{ years (peace + physical survival + parental love)} +$$
$$3 \text{ years (chaos + emotional survival + independence)}$$
$$\text{with God encompassing the whole equation} = ME$$

Even though it was defined by two totally diverse factors, I understood the equation. I was able to accept it and make it work.

Then came the ninth year of my life and a furlough trip to the United States. During that year a decision was made that our family would not return to Africa. Until the doctors determined that my younger brother was well enough, we would have to remain in the

United States — a place where neither my mom nor my two brothers and I felt at home. (Bupah, who had grown up in America, made the adjustment much more easily.)

Uncomfortable as I was, I decided to make the most of it. I entered the life of public school education with enthusiasm. I was a good student and an even better athlete. That's how I ended up on the cement playground at Ventnor Avenue Elementary School that day.

We were playing dodge ball. My friend, Paula, and I had been invited to join the boys. We were the only two girls who could keep up with them, and they needed a few more players to even up the sides. The game was rather lethargic, so Paula and I carried on a conversation as we dodged the large, red, rubber ball. In the course of that conversation I mentioned something about God. I don't have any recollection of why He was part of the discussion. What I vividly remember, however, is her response: "How do you even know there is a God?"

I stopped dodging the ball and stood still in disbelief. It was the first time in my life that anyone had questioned God's existence. It was a question I had never even contemplated coming from the lips of a human being. It startled me. So did the red rubber ball as it whacked me upside the head, imbedding Paula's question permanently in my brain.

I was silent for a long time, but as we headed up the steps to our classroom, I replied very emphatically, "Because there is! That's why!" She looked at me strangely, but my answer seemed to satisfy her. She never again questioned God's existence — at least not in my presence. But the answer didn't satisfy *me*. There remained a question mark in my brain that could not be dislodged.

I began to search for the answer, but no one seemed to have it. My parents quoted Scripture. Sunday school teachers pointed to the Bible. Family friends shrugged their shoulders. But no one was able to explain why or how the Bible became the ultimate source for all answers. *Couldn't it be just another "Greek-type" myth book?* I wondered as I got into junior high and began to study mythology. They laughed at my inquisitive but ignorant mind. Surprisingly, when I questioned some of my public school teachers, I found they held to Paula's view that perhaps there wasn't any God at all.

I was terribly confused. Maybe there really wasn't a God. But if there wasn't, what *was* there? How did we get here? What was life all about? Why had my parents even gone to Africa? ("Because God sent us, dear," they replied, not realizing His very existence was in jeopardy in my mind.) Ultimately I questioned — *who* and *why* was I?

There followed a series of events in my life that added question upon question to the ones already mounting in my brain. We had to move. We had no place to live while my dad (Bupah) hunted for a job. The only place we could afford was a small basement apartment — one room for five people to live and grow in. *Couldn't God, if He did exist, take better care of my family than this?*

Finally Bupah found a wonderful job as the pastor of a beautiful country church in Pennsylvania. Life was fine again. The questions spun themselves to the back of my brain where they rested — for two short years — until Bupah became ill, so ill that he could not prepare a sermon. His illness was permanent and devastating — it was Alzheimer's disease. Hungry days followed, lean years when only two skirts, one blouse, and one pair of shoes were all that could be found in my closet.

Could Paula have been right? If there was a God, wouldn't He take extra good care of a man who had given up everything, including a promising job with IBM, to go to the mission field to serve Him? Yet there sat my dad on the couch turning into a vegetable while his God looked on from a distance.

And speaking of the mission field, I began to worry, what happens to the people in those faraway places who never hear about Jesus, the ones the missionaries never get to? Many of the people in the villages my parents entered had never seen or heard of a Bible, let alone read one. And there were many other villages we didn't dare enter. How did those villagers stand a chance if Jesus was the only way to heaven?

My brain was about to explode. I finally approached an elder in the church we attended. After bombarding him with all my questions and doubts, he stood there speechless, flabbergasted — much as I had in the cement schoolyard a few years before. Then he declared to the whole world that I was an insolent, faithless teenager who was totally unworthy of God's love. (He obviously didn't know the answers either!)

It wasn't until I arrived at college that I began to find answers to my questions. They came in the form of a book assigned by an archaeology professor at the University of Pennsylvania. It was titled *The Psychology of Religious Experience,* by Dr. Erwin P. Goodenough (yep, that was his name), and it answered most of my questions with one simple answer. It explained that Christianity, just like all other world religions, is a crutch — a wonderful, psychological crutch that helps people through life. The biblical account of Christianity, it continued to explain, is no more accurate or true than the story of *The Three Bears,* and no more harmful — unless it is imposed on others. This explanation made perfect sense to me at the moment. It allowed my brain to rest after years of tormenting itself with spiritual questions. I accepted it wholeheartedly. I also decided that I was strong enough not to need such a crutch. I would make it the rest of the way through life on my own, without God or religion.

But the God I dismissed did not dismiss me. He, with His wonderful wit and wisdom, which I have since come to understand and enjoy, caused me to fall in love with a man who was just on the verge of coming to a personal belief in God for the first time in his life. I tried to dissuade him, but soon decided that if he needed such a crutch I should not be the one to kick it out from underneath him. "To each his own method of hobbling through life" became my philosophy.

We were married just before our senior year of college, during which he announced that he would like to go to seminary when he graduated. I about choked on the thought, but he promised me that he would not spend his life in the ministry. He just wanted answers to some questions. Fine. I certainly understood the need for answers. He was obviously just a little tardier in going through the process than I had been.

Since I enjoyed writing, my new husband (who later became your dad) often called on me to help him with his seminary papers. Together we deciphered long passages of Scripture and read the commentaries of wise men. I wasn't looking for answers anymore. I had the one that I needed. But it wasn't long before the possibility dawned on me that perhaps my search had not been complete. Maybe there really *were* answers from a "Christian" point of view. Once again I was confused, but God began leading people into my life whose wisdom and kindness drew me back to the message I had abandoned and the God I had denied.

All the answers to the myriad of questions I raised did not come at once. But knowing that there *were* answers satisfied my soul and gave it rest. The only thing left troubling me was that *so* many Christians were *so* ignorant of their faith.

Five years into our marriage and about two years into my

blossoming faith, you guys started coming along — first baby Zach, followed by Matthew, Ben, and Jonathan — again the perfect result of God's wit and wisdom. (I had no intention of bringing children into an already overpopulated, ill-mannered world. God had other plans!) Once the task was assigned and I realized how privileged I was, I took on the responsibility of raising you with tremendous joy and enthusiasm.

As Dad entered the ministry full-time (there's that heavenly sense of humor again), God led him to Search Ministries, where years had already been spent researching answers to the very questions that had bothered me most of my growing-up life. It was part of Dad's job to help me answer them. How ironic, how just like God!

Now that you are entering your adolescent years, sure enough each of you has begun to raise the same questions I so desperately sought to resolve as a preteen and teenager. Your questions *are* valid. And a biblical faith *is* defensible. As your mom, I am obligated to find answers that make it reasonable in your eyes. My ongoing search is the basis for this book. First Peter 3:15 says, "Always be prepared to give an answer to everyone who asks you to give the reason for the hope that you have." Here are some of the *reasons* for the hope that we share.

QUESTION #1

CAN YOU PROVE TO ME
That There Is a God?

THEY SAY THAT ANYONE BORN IN TEXAS WILL CONSIDER HIMSELF A TEXAN for the rest of his life. I guess it's true! Zach only lived in Texas a few months before we grabbed him out of his cradle and transported him to Portland, Oregon. Then we lugged him across the country to Georgia before we finally settled in Central Florida.

Zach has sampled just about every section of the United States, but he has always loved "going home" to Texas. His roots, tiny as they were when we dug them up, seem to crave the fertile soil of the Lone Star State.

I'll never forget the first time we returned to Texas with Zach. He was probably too young to remember the long trip we made through the rolling hills in the eastern part of the state and across the vast plains into central Texas to visit some friends. They had just built a huge house in a brand-new subdivision in the middle of nowhere. There wasn't a tree in sight.

Zach was not used to such a landscape. All the houses we ever owned were surrounded by towering trees. The evergreen trees in

Oregon rose eighty feet or so above our house. They creaked and moaned and swayed their branches every time a storm blew through. Then we found ourselves on the edge of a forested belt-way near Atlanta, where you all enjoyed plenty of climbing adventures. Even now, the oak trees that line our street in Florida are magnificent. A single tree provides shade for our entire backyard!

Zach seemed puzzled by the stark Texas scenery that day, but soon he ran off to play with his new friends. About forty minutes later, storm clouds began to gather, and we called him in. The wind kicked up and started swirling the dust in little whirlwinds across the bleak terrain. Zach stood on the porch staring across the fields with wide, wonder-filled eyes. Finally he wondered out loud, "Mommy, how can the wind blow when there aren't any trees?"

It took me awhile to decipher the dilemma in his mind, but I finally caught on. Wind had always been associated with trees in his life. Every time the wind had blown, the trees in our yards had moved their leaves or swayed their branches. From his observations, Zach had concluded that it was the movement of the trees, acting like large fans, which caused the wind to blow, rather than vice versa! If just the leaves moved, they stirred up a gentle breeze, but if the trees chose to exercise their limbs completely, a full-blown hurricane could occur! Obviously his young mind had transposed the cause and effect.

You have asked me if I can prove to you that there is a God. Based on Zach's experience in Texas, let me ask you a similar question: *Can you prove to me that there is wind?*

You can't, can you — at least not scientifically. Wind is not observable. It can't be captured and placed in a jar and set free to blow again. All you can do is study its effects. (I presume that you understand the process a little better now than Zach did when he was four years old!) By studying the data surrounding wind, you can provide proof that it really does exist, and your evidence will hold up in any court of law.

In the same way, I cannot prove to you scientifically that there is a God. But I can give you plenty of evidence for His existence based on the effects we see in our universe and in our own lives. Hopefully, you will reach the same conclusion about God's reality that you have about the wind. Here are five indisputable facts:

1. The universe exists, and something had to bring it into existence (the argument of **sufficient cause**).

If I insisted that the baseball field down at the Little League park just happened to appear naturally over the course of time, would you believe me? Would it make sense to you that squirrels running back and forth to collect acorns formed the base paths? Would you agree with my conclusion that, although red clay does not occur naturally in central Florida, it just happened to surface between the squirrels' diamond-shaped paths and gophers then burrowed the clay into a mound? Could you accept the explanation that some wire must have fallen off a big truck traveling along the highway, and the wind blew it until it unrolled to form a fence around the perimeter? I'm sure you'd agree that the dugouts are in such bad shape that they very possibly *were* the result of rain and mud forming clumps of cement!

Anyway, you get the point. There's no way you'd believe any of that. Right? (Instead you'd assume that my brain was beginning to deteriorate!) Squirrels and wind and rain are not *sufficient cause* to justify the existence of a baseball field in the middle of a bunch of scrub brush. Any sane individual understands this.

Well, the constantly moving, ever-expanding, highly organized universe we live in had to have a *sufficient cause* as well. There has to be an explanation for where it all came from. It couldn't have just showed up by accident over eons of time. Something had to at least get it started.

"Why couldn't it have just caused itself to begin?" you might ask.

"Oh, you're referring to something like a 'big bang' that might have suddenly started it all," I would acknowledge. As you nodded I would quickly ask, "Then what caused the 'big bang?'"

And you'd probably shrug, and say something like, "Nothing — it just happened!"

If I suddenly heard an explosion in the backyard, and I asked you what happened, do you think I would believe you if you said, "Nothing!"? Not for one second! Something had to cause the bang. Never in the history of mankind's existence has something (a noise, a smell, a taste, an object — anything!) appeared out of nothing. According to all our scientific discoveries and laws, that is impossible!

So how did it all get started? Where did the universe come from — whether it was spoken, banged, or oozed into existence?

There has to be something different from everything else in the universe — something that existed on its own before anything else began, something that itself was uncaused — that caused everything else to begin. The *sufficient cause* of our universe must exist outside of our universe and it must be eternal!

If you're confused, you're not the only one. This problem nagged Dr. Allan Sandage, winner of the 1999 Crafoord Prize for Astronomy (the equivalent of a Nobel Prize) for many years. Although he was an avowed atheist (he didn't believe in the existence of God), the question of the origin of the universe bothered him from his youth. "Why is there something rather than nothing?" he wondered as he stared at the galaxies through his telescope, continuing the research begun by Dr. Edwin Hubble.

At the age of fifty, Dr. Sandage finally concluded that there must be a Supreme Being of some sort who set our universe in motion. "It was my science that drove me to the conclusion that the world is much more complicated than can be explained by science," he is quoted as saying. "It is only through the supernatural that I can understand the mystery of existence."[1] Later he came to identify that Supreme Being as the God of the Bible. It was his observation of nature and the conclusion that all effects must have a cause that led this great scientific mind to a concrete belief in a sovereign God.

2. The universe not only exists, it is constantly moving and expanding (the argument of **motion**).

I mentioned a couple of paragraphs back that our highly organized universe is constantly on the move. Let's think for a minute about movement in terms of going bowling. You could set a bowling ball at the end of the alley and wait all night for it to roll down the lane by itself, and it would never budge. Someone (or something — like maybe an earthquake) has to get it started. You see, another argument from science, which leads us to believe that an outside agent must have been involved in the existence of the universe, is the argument of motion. Something immobile cannot suddenly move without some kind of shove. Something has to start it in motion.

"Wait a minute," you might object. "*I* move *myself*. Nobody has to push me out of bed in the morning — well, at least most mornings. See, my body moves all by itself." (I can picture you flexing your muscles or making some kind of spastic motions at this point.)

"Actually, it doesn't!" I would reply. "Your mind moves your body." Your physical body cannot move by itself. Did you ever see a dead man move, except in a science fiction horror-thriller? I don't think so! A physical object has no ability to move on its own. Something outside the realm of the *physical* has to cause motion.

If you've followed my reasoning so far, you'll understand that something outside the universe had to bring it into existence, and something had to set it in motion. There had to be *sufficient cause* for both existence and motion. And as we've already said, that *sufficient cause* had to be *eternal.*

3. All design must have a designer

(the argument of **design**).

Remember that baseball diamond we mentioned earlier? No matter how brilliant the squirrels or gophers are in Florida nor how strong the wind can blow here, a ball field can't just come into existence on its own. Its angles and measurements indicate that someone with a lot of intelligence had to design and engineer it.

Nature is not filled with haphazard creatures and random events. It is filled with incredible, intricate design. And design always points to a designer. The seasons, the tides, the sequences and rhythms operating within our bodies all point to unimaginable intelligence.

Look at your CD player. All the component parts are designed to work together for a specific purpose — basically so that you can play CDs and torment your parents with loud music! The more you study its parts, the more you can appreciate the fact that intelligence, purpose, and design are necessary to produce a CD player. Someone didn't just throw a bunch of pieces of equipment in a box one day, shake it up, and *voilà*, there was your CD player.

Chance cannot produce intelligence. Accidents cannot produce purpose. Chaos cannot produce order. No, the effect cannot be greater than the cause. Yet your CD player is nothing compared to the complexity of one living cell. Given time and chance cells could not have just evolved by themselves.

Would you want to get on an airplane if you knew the flight computer had been programmed by a horde of grasshoppers that started hopping up and down and randomly chomping on computer chips in order to configure them? (I'm talking *really* tiny grasshoppers with *really* strong teeth, here!) No, the task is far too complex and intricate to hope they could get even one sequence correct. So how could anyone ever presume that time and chance allowed our brains and nervous systems to be programmed into systems far more complex than the most intricate computer that has ever been designed?

4. We universally praise certain values
   (the argument of **morality**).

Another proof of the existence of a Supreme Being who designed a tremendously complex universe can be argued from the standpoint of morality. Certainly you would agree that we view some things in this world as being better than others. Universally we seem to agree that love is better than hate, peace is better than war, people are better than broccoli. (At least *most* people.) And with very few exceptions, every culture throughout history has prized qualities such as honesty, wisdom, courage, and fairness as virtues.

When we believe that certain things are "better" than others, we are admitting that we believe in a standard of goodness against which we are willing to measure these attributes. The fact that we allow ourselves to make moral judgments at all implies that we believe in the existence of an "Absolute Good" — a "Best" which nothing can supersede.

5. Personal beings could not have been created by an impersonal force (the argument of **personality**).

Nothing impersonal has ever been known to produce anything personal. Although it can reflect personality, an impersonal piece of marble never chiseled a statue of George Washington from itself. Although it definitely can depict emotion, an impersonal piece of canvas never painted a portrait of the Mona Lisa. No, quite the opposite is true. When a marble statue or a canvas portrait reflects personality, it proves that a personal being made it. The fact that it exists implies the existence of the artist who created it.

If you were walking along the beach early one morning and saw a large heart-shaped picture scuffed in the sand with the words *Kevin loves Kristen* printed in seashells, you wouldn't think, "Oh, look what happened when the tide washed in last night! Some seashells were swept in, and they left a perfect little message. Then this morning, when the tide went back out, some crabs scuttling for food must have formed a big heart shape around it!"

No! You'd think, "Someone got down to the beach this morning before I did and is trying to steal my girlfriend!"

Simple designs can be created on the beach by blowing wind or rippling water, but designs that reflect intelligence and personality can only be created by an intelligent, personal designer. (Not necessarily extremely intelligent if he's trying to steal your girlfriend!)

The universe contains people with personalities — some better than others. We have minds, emotions, and wills. We could not be the products of an impersonal universe. Our designer must have been able to think, feel, and choose or he would have been inferior to his created, conscious, personal beings. And as I said before, the effect cannot be greater than the cause. Therefore, the eternally existing, ethically good designer, who caused the universe to come into existence, must also be personal.

NEED MORE PROOF?

Maybe you are still not convinced. Let me make one more point. Suppose the large circle on this page represents all the knowledge of the universe. The smaller circle within it represents all the knowledge that humankind has been able to discover so far through all the ages of our existence. I want you to draw another circle within this circle to represent what *you* know — your own personal knowledge. If you are honest, your circle is probably a minute dot. Regardless, I'm sure you did not fill up the entire circle. There should be a lot of space left over.

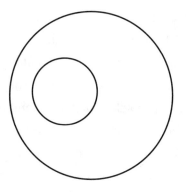

I mentioned that I was raised in Nigeria, West Africa, where Granny and Bupah were missionaries. The village we lived in was very primitive. We had no electricity or running water. We cooked on a wood-burning stove, and for years we washed our clothes in a big, metal bucket. Then one day your Bupah acquired a gasoline refrigerator and a gas-powered washing machine. You should have seen the villagers' faces as he tried to explain these two mechanical devices. (The lawn mower he later brought home was an even greater dilemma to them. It was a horrifying, roaring monster that ate the grass and spit it out!)

However, the concept they had the most trouble comprehending was ice. They refused to believe that our new gas refrigerator with the tiny freezer could possibly make water hard. They just shook their heads at our ignorant boastings. When we tried to describe whole rivers and lakes hard enough to walk on, they laughed out loud. It wasn't until we placed little cubes in their hands and allowed them to melt back into water that they began to accept the idea that ice could really exist. Up to that point it had been outside their sphere of knowledge. But did their ignorance and lack of belief in any way jeopardize the existence of ice? No, not one bit.

Look back at the circle you drew. Since you, and all the rest of humanity, are obviously ignorant of some knowledge, isn't it true that God could exist somewhere outside the scope of your comprehension? You have to admit that this is true, or you are claiming to be omniscient — that you know everything there is to know.

I cannot prove to you scientifically beyond a shadow of doubt that God exists, but I ask you to weigh your options. What if He doesn't exist and you believe He does? What harm has it done? But what if He does exist . . . and you don't believe? Wow!

Look at it this way. Suppose you are diagnosed with a dreadful disease. Without an operation you have no chance of survival. Suppose a surgeon promises you a 50/50 chance to live if he operates. Would you agree to have the operation? If you didn't, I, as your mom, would no doubt immediately overrule, and you'd be on a gurney headed for the operating room first thing in the morning!

The true weight of the evidence in favor of the existence of a God based on cause and effect, order and design, as well as your own personality and sense of morality, makes it far greater than a 50/50 proposition. And the consequences of not accepting His existence are far graver than physical death.

Just as you cannot prove to me that the wind really blew that day in Texas, kicking the dust into Zach's face, I cannot prove to you that there is a God. I can only show you His effects on our universe and in your life, and offer you *sufficient cause* to believe. Please check it all out carefully. I want you to understand that there is overwhelming evidence to support that there really is a God.

SUMMARY

Although I cannot prove God's existence by showing Him to you any more than you can show me the wind, I can present you with five indisputable facts that provide overwhelming proof of His existence:

1. The universe exists, and something had to bring it into existence.
2. The universe not only exists, it is constantly moving and expanding. Something had to put it in motion.
3. All design must have a designer.
4. We universally praise certain values as better than others, pointing to the existence of an Ultimate Good or Best.
5. Personal beings could not have been created by an impersonal force.

Also, you cannot claim to know everything there is to know. The fact that something exists outside the limits of our knowledge does not in any way invalidate its existence.

After examining the evidence, the only wise and prudent choice is to accept the existence of a Supreme Being who created the universe, set it in motion, and gave it personality. The Bible calls Him God.

QUESTION #2

IF THERE IS A GOD, WHY DOES *He Allow So Much Suffering?*

THIS IS A GREAT QUESTION, ONE THAT HAS TRIPPED UP MANY PEOPLE IN their search for spiritual truth. I presume that as you ask it you are presupposing, as most people do, that in order to *be* God, this Being must be totally good and completely powerful. Yet when you look around, you observe evil, painful, terrible things happening. The newspaper just this morning was filled with suffering and death and injustice. You can think of two options: (1) If there really is a God running the show, and He really is all-powerful, He must want these bad things to happen since He allows them. But that would make Him less than good. Or (2) if He doesn't want them to happen, and they do anyway, then He cannot be all-powerful. This creates quite a dilemma.

There are two questions we need to answer if we are going to attempt to find a solution for this dilemma: (1) What is the source of these terrible, painful happenings? In other words — where does evil come from? and (2) When will evil end? Let's take them one at a time:

1. WHERE DOES EVIL COME FROM?

Several years ago Zach and MattE were fishing in the pond behind the house. Before long they got in a big argument over bait. Zach quickly grew tired of Matthew (MattE) pilfering from the pile of freshwater clams he had spent all morning digging up. So the next time MattE reached over to sneak one, Zach picked up a stick and swung it to protect his property. He swears to this day that he had no idea that his younger brother would bend over at exactly that moment, putting his stick and MattE's nose on a collision course. But that's what happened, and MattE ran home with blood dripping down his face and onto his shirt.

It was wrong (evil) of Zach to hit MattE, right? No argument there. Was the stick that struck MattE's nose evil? No, as a matter of fact, at the time Zach thought it was a pretty good stick. Was the hand that swung the stick evil? No, if we had cut it off and placed it on the table it couldn't have done anything good or bad (except perhaps bleed all over the new tablecloth!). A hand by itself is neither good nor evil. Then what was evil in this case? Zach's choice to swing the stick was evil. God did not make that choice, therefore God did not make the evil act. Zach did.

I know what you're thinking by the challenging look in your eyes. You're thinking, "Hmph, if God didn't make that choice, then God didn't make *every*thing." But here's where you're wrong. God did make every *thing*. Did you catch the difference? Evil is not a created *thing* that can exist on its own. It is real, but it can only exist in the absence of its created opposite, which is *good*. You may not like all this philosophical stuff, but try to hang in there for just one more minute.

This illustration might help. Remember the old, wooden picnic table that used to sit in our backyard? It rotted and started to fall apart, so we threw it away. Now, the rot that ate away at the table could not have existed without the table itself. That's because there is no such thing as a perfect state of "rotted-ness." A perfectly (completely) rotten picnic table would cease to exist. The same is true of rust. If our neighbor's old gray Cadillac rusts much more, it will completely disappear off the face of the planet. Rust cannot exist on its own. Rot, rust, evil — these things are called *privations.* You don't have to remember the big word. Just remember that evil only exists as a corruption of some good thing. It has no essence (or existence) by itself.

Let's use another story as an example. This time let's put Matthew on the spot instead of Zach. When he was about five years old, MattE received a huge Styrofoam airplane for his birthday. It had to be assembled, and it came with detailed instructions. He could hardly wait to go outside to fly it, so he started jamming pieces together. I grabbed the instructions and sat down beside him to try and help before he ruined it completely. We finally got it together, except for one minor detail. There was one wing with a blue tip and one with a red tip. The blue-tipped wing was supposed to go into the slot that was painted blue, and of course, the red one was supposed to go into the red slot. But MattE didn't like it that way. He thought it looked more like a cool flying machine if the wings were reversed. I couldn't convince him otherwise, so off he went to the hill beside our house with the wings in backward. Sure enough, on its maiden voyage the airplane crashed and broke into several pieces.

The potential for that airplane to break apart existed from the very beginning. The designer had given specific instructions on how to use it properly and had even warned of the consequences if those instructions weren't followed. Whose fault was it that the airplane broke? Yep, the little boy with the big, brown eyes and the tears running down his face. (Thank goodness for duct tape!)

God created you and me, but He created us with a free will to make our own decisions; to choose to follow His instructions or to ignore them; to do good or to do evil. If we didn't have free choice — and could do only good — we would be no more than robots or puppets. We would have no need for our minds, or our wills, or our emotions. We would have no personality or capacity to love. We must be given the option to choose *not* to love in order for real love to be possible. Do you understand? Love demands a choice.

Unfortunately, when we are given a choice, the potential exists for making the wrong one. But is it the Designer's fault when we do? He has given us specific instructions on how to live life properly and has even warned us of the consequences if we don't. Whose fault is it when we make an evil decision? It can only be our own.

I don't know if you've noticed or not, but so far I've given you only the answer to why *moral* evil exists — the type of evil one man chooses to inflict on another. But what about suffering caused naturally — like birth defects, tornadoes, illnesses, and epidemics — the things man has no control over, things that would fit into a category called *natural* evil?

When God created the world, it was perfect — man, the animals, the earth, the universe (see Genesis 1:31). The setting in which He chose to place man was the perfect Garden of Eden. But once again — here's the love part — since God loved Adam, He gave Adam the opportunity to choose to love Him back. When Adam and Eve decided to disobey instead, they started mankind down a path that included suffering (see Genesis 3). Disease, defects, and disasters of nature are all physical results of man's spiritual choice to take the path that leads away from God.

All choices have consequences. If they didn't, there would be no choice involved. The more significant the choice, the greater the consequences. For example, the choice to drink a Coke or a Pepsi is relatively insignificant and so are the consequences. Choosing Coke versus coffee is only slightly more significant, but once again, the consequences are not substantial. However, choosing to drink a glass of Coke or a glass of Clorox is extremely signifi-cant, and the consequences are serious. Adam's choice to obey or disobey God was the most significant choice he could ever face. Therefore, the consequences were extremely severe.

When I was about eleven years old, I spent a week with my cousin who lived in the country in upstate New York. Since I was a tomboy I enjoyed playing in the fields and along the streams that bordered her property. But one day I decided that it would be nice to head into town. She informed me that it was about a ten-mile trek along a country road. I knew that the road wound its way down the mountain, and I figured that if we cut through the woods and met it on the other side, we could shorten the journey by at least three miles. Missy wasn't very excited about the prospect, but I pointed out a path that headed into the woods, and she reluctantly decided to join me.

So off we headed on our shortcut. At first our adventure was exciting, but as we traveled deeper into the woods the underbrush grew thicker and the path became narrow. At one point Missy tripped over a vine and hit her head on a tree trunk. Needless to say, she was not at all happy after that, even when I insisted that the knot on her forehead would go down before we reached town.

Looking around, I realized that just about every tree and shrub was covered with poison ivy. Missy began to itch, but I urged her on. When we came to a small stream, I jumped over it and landed on a loose rock, twisting my ankle. A snake slithered out from under the rock. At that point Missy became hysterical, and I decided it was time to turn around. There was a small problem, however. I couldn't even begin to find the trail back.

After hours of wandering (and listening to Missy whimpering) we came to a clearing. Joy of all joys, there, across the small field, was a man fixing a fence. We ran and limped to him as fast as we could, and he directed two forlorn, beat-up little girls to the country road — which had only been a few hundred yards away the whole time. We had definitely made an unwise choice when we took the path through the woods, but we were over-joyed when we finally reached the paved country road that would take us home.

The path Adam and Eve chose was not the one God had in mind. The road God had intended was smooth and pleasant. The shortcut they unwisely chose, however, was covered with poison ivy that would torment them, rocks that would trip them, and snakes that would bite them. Children were born to Adam and Eve as they traveled their chosen path. Then children were born to their children; more children were born to those children; and so on and so on until it gets to us. We (and everyone else) are stuck on that path through the woods. It's all part of the conse-quence for the extremely significant choice Adam and Eve made.

It's not fair, is it? Or at least it wouldn't be if the story ended there. Why doesn't God put another fork in our path and allow us each to make our own choice to go back to the paved, smooth road and get off this course of suffering?

That's exactly what He does. He sent His son Jesus to show us the way to the perfect road — to give us a choice to get back on it, away from the suffering and evil of the supposed shortcut through the woods. Everyone has the chance and the choice to accept Him as Savior, the One who will get them off this tortuous path. If we make that choice, we will be guided through this present, cursed, suffering world into an eternity of nonsuffering perfection.

2. WHEN WILL EVIL END?

We've established that God does not *cause* evil. But He *allows* it. But isn't allowing evil just as bad as causing it? How can He continue allowing airplanes to crash, killing hundreds of people, and floods to wipe out whole towns? Why does He allow ethnic atrocities to occur all over our globe? Why are so many people allowed to suffer from cancer? Why, if He is all-powerful, doesn't He stop all pain and suffering right now?

If God chose to wipe out all suffering right now, He'd have to wipe out the cause of all suffering. Since every person on earth causes some degree of suffering at some point (because we all make choices that are disobedient to God), we would all have to be wiped out. Humankind would be eradicated from the universe.

However, there *will* come a time when God chooses to do away with all evil — a time when He yells, "That's it. Time's up. I've had enough!" Anyone still on the dirt path headed deeper into the woods will be forced to stay on that tortuous path forever. They will suffer eternal separation from God. (Remember, it was their choice.) Those who have chosen to head back to the paved road will be immediately escorted home to live in an eternally perfect place prepared for them by God. (You can read about this in 2 Peter 3:7-13 and Revelation 21:4; 22:3-7.)

I mentioned to you that this question is one that trips up many people in their search for spiritual truth. That's because one of the premises they make in trying to answer it is incorrect, therefore making it impossible for them to come to the right conclusion. Several prominent atheistic thinkers like David Hume, H. G. Wells, and Bertrand Russell reasoned it this way:

If God is all-good, He will destroy evil.
If God is all-powerful, He can destroy evil.

Evil is not destroyed.

Therefore, there is no all-good, all-powerful God.

Their reasoning was completely wrong because they left out one crucial word. Let's restate the dilemma and its conclusion correctly:

If God is all-good, He will destroy evil.

If God is all-powerful, He can destroy evil.

Evil is not destroyed *YET*.

But evil will be destroyed one day by this all-good,

all-powerful God.

Peter, in 2 Peter 3:9, explains that God, in His love, is being patient. He wants to give as many people as possible a chance to repent — to make the choice to get on the right path. Let me ask you this: What if God had decided to put an end to all evil the night before you made the decision to accept Jesus as your Savior? Where would you be right now?

SUMMARY

God created a perfect universe without evil and suffering. He also created man as a perfect being, but with the ability to choose freely to love or reject his Maker. Adam (I must admit here that Eve was every bit as involved as Adam) chose to reject God's perfect plan, and therefore they started us all on a path full of *natural* suffering and pain that will only be relieved when we get to heaven.

Each day we are faced with choices that have consequences. Because God loves us and wants our love in return, He allows us to choose whether or not we will follow His instructions. If we choose not to obey Him (evil), then we are to blame for the *moral* consequences, not God. Evil is not some *thing* He has created. Evil is a result of our wrong choices.

God allows suffering to continue so that more people can have the opportunity to accept Christ and escape eternal suffering. He has promised that one day He will ultimately destroy evil. Then we, who have made the choice to accept Christ as our Savior, will live with Him in an eternally perfect world free from all suffering and pain. Wow! It's hard to even imagine the beauty and the peace. Won't it be wonderful?

QUESTION #3

How Do We Know That the
Bible Is a Reliable Source?

Good question! And the answer to it is critical! Christians say the Bible is the authority for everything they claim to believe. But how can we be sure that *God* really told certain people what to write down — that they didn't just make it all up? *And,* if the words they wrote *were* given to them by God, are the texts we now have accurate versions of what they originally wrote? If we can't find answers to both of these questions, could it be possible that we are just victims of a giant hoax?

Fortunately, there is much evidence to uphold the integrity of the Bible, proving that it is not only a reliable document but also more than just the product of human minds and human hands. Let's start by examining the Bible in light of history and archaeology.

THE EVIDENCE OF HISTORICAL AND ARCHAEOLOGICAL ACCURACY

Once, several years ago, I got very upset with Ben for leaving the back gate open and letting the dog out. He tried, but there was no way he could convince me that he had closed the gate and that our tiny Boston terrier had gotten out on his own. The evidence proved otherwise.

"King couldn't have reached the latch even if he turned his water bucket over, dragged it to the gate, and stood on it," I reasoned a little sarcastically. "Plus, even if he had done all that, somehow he would have had to remove the metal pin from the slot before he could lift the latch. It's impossible," I concluded.

Ben was insistent that he had acted responsibly by closing the gate. I was convinced that he had been careless . . . until the next day when I put King in the backyard myself. I shut the gate and put the pin in the latch. Less than a half hour later he was scratching at the front door. I was baffled. I put him back in the yard again and watched from the window. What I saw astonished me. That little critter pulled himself up on the chain link fence like a monkey, removed the pin with his teeth, and pushed on the latch with his pug nose. The gate swung open. Sure enough, he was able to set himself free. I was amazed, but as incredible as it was, I could no longer doubt Ben's story.

The same thing happens over and over with people, places, and events mentioned in the Bible. Scholars insist "they never existed," or "that couldn't have happened," or "the biblical time frame is historically incorrect." But over and over, archaeological discoveries prove otherwise. Everything that has been discovered, uncovered, and checked out shows that the biblical account is accurate. Often it's amazing, but seldom do the archaeological findings leave any doubt.

Take for example the Hittite Empire mentioned several times in the Old Testament (see Genesis 10:15; 23:10; Judges 1:26; 1 Samuel 26:6; Ezekiel 16:3). Scholars refused to believe that such an empire ever existed because it was mentioned nowhere else in history. Then, in 1906, the Hittite capital was unearthed.[1]

For years scholars questioned the accuracy of Daniel chapter 5, in which Belshazzar is named as the king of Babylon. All their archaeological records said that Nabonidus was king at that time. There was no reference whatsoever to any King Belshazzar anywhere — until 1965 when three inscribed stone slabs were discovered in Haran. They cleared up the problem showing that King Nabonidus had assigned kingly duties to his son Belshazzar while he went off to fight the Persians. The dates showed clearly that this took place during the time that Daniel wrote.[2]

Luke's gospel account of Lysanias as the "tetrarch of Abilene" (Luke 3:1) was highly criticized until archaeologists recently found two Greek inscriptions that prove Lysanias really was the tetrarch of Abilene from A.D. 14 to A.D. 29.[3]

Most of the New Testament was written between A.D. 47 and A.D. 70, and all of it was completed before the end of the first century. Many eyewitnesses to the accounts were still alive when the books were first circulated. They could have easily challenged any fictitious accounts of the life of Jesus Christ. Instead, extrabiblical writings by early Roman, Greek, and Jewish sources verify the major details of the New Testament. Flavius Josephus, a Jewish historian and commander of Jewish forces in Galilee in A.D. 66, made specific references to the baptisms that John the Baptist performed in the Jordan River and his death at the hands of Herod. He spoke of Jesus Christ and James in his writings.[4] He also mentions the Pharisees and Sadducees, Annas and Caiaphas (whom Jesus stood before when He was on trial), and the Roman emperors who are written about in the Gospels and the book of Acts. Governors and satirists, as well as historians, wrote about Jesus Christ. A description of His death was included in a personal letter (preserved in the British Museum) from an imprisoned Syrian to his son around A.D. 73.[5]

No archaeological finding has ever contradicted the biblical account. On the contrary, archaeological studies continue to authenticate and validate the historicity and accuracy of the Bible. Let's look at some other evidences that validate the Bible as a reliable source.

THE EVIDENCE OF UNITY

Suppose all four of you got in a fight — not that this has ever really happened before. (Yeah, right!) As part of your punishment, suppose I asked each of you to sit down and write a two-page paper describing what happened. How similar do you think those accounts would be? I imagine I would have at least two different versions of who started the fight, three different accounts of why, and four different analyses of who won the fight and who should be punished the most. I'm sure very little unity of opinion would exist in any of those two-page papers.

Well, the Bible was written over a period of 1,500 years, in 66 volumes, by more than 40 different people from widely varied backgrounds, living on three different continents (Europe, Asia, and North Africa), using three different languages (Hebrew, Greek, and Aramaic). Yet despite this incredible diversity, and often while dealing with controversial subject material, they wrote in complete accord. There is one harmonious, consistent message from the beginning to the end — the redemption of humanity by God through the person and work of Jesus Christ. This is an incredible feat!

Just think about it. Moses was a well-educated political leader. Joshua was a military general. Solomon was a king, Daniel a prime minister, and Ezra a priest. Amos herded goats, Peter caught fish, and Matthew collected taxes. There was a shepherd, a doctor, and a rabbi. They were rich, poor, young, old, educated, and uneducated. They were from all walks of life. Yet the main theme and continuous message of the entire Bible is salvation through Jesus Christ. It cannot be explained that so many different personalities, living in so many different cultures, at such vastly different times, wrote in such complete accord, except as Peter explains it in 2 Peter 1:21, NASB: "Men moved by the Holy Spirit spoke from God." No, this feat would not have been possible if one and the same God had not inspired them.

You know, I can't even get all four of you to agree on where we should go out for dinner. That's why we usually end up at a food court in the mall where there are lots of options!

THE EVIDENCE OF FULFILLED PROPHECY

Did you know that about one quarter of the Bible was unfulfilled prophecy at the time it was written? Yet everything happened, or is happening, just the way the Bible predicted it would. In the book of Genesis, Abraham was promised that his descendants would never be wiped out. Today the Arabs (descendants of his first son, Ishmael) and the Jews (descendants of his second son, Isaac) are still distinct people. However, there are no Edomites, Assyrians, Babylonians, Medes, or Canaanites. Did you ever wonder why? It's because the Bible promises in Genesis 12:2-3 that anyone who curses the Israelites will be cursed by God. These people, who harassed and tortured the seed of Abraham, have been wiped out of existence along with Adolph Hitler, his Third Reich, and many more.

Daniel predicted the rise and fall of Babylon, Persia, Greece, and Rome long before they ever took place. Ezekiel, writing during the sixth century B.C., prophesied the destruction of the city of Tyre (see Ezekiel 26), which took place in 332 B.C. At the time of Ezekiel's prediction, Tyre was a prominent Phoenician seaport. Part of the city was on the mainland and part was built on an island a half mile off the coast. Ezekiel prophesied that Nebuchadnezzar would besiege the city and destroy it, that many nations would come against it, that the ruins would be scraped from the site and thrown into the sea, leaving nothing but a bare rock where fishermen would spread their nets. He said the city would never be rebuilt. Every detail of Ezekiel's prophecy was fulfilled. Nebuchadnezzar besieged the mainland city for thirteen years starting in 586 B.C., and finally destroyed it. The island city remained intact, however, until Alexander the Great came along in 332 B.C. and overthrew it. The only way he could get to it, though, was by building a causeway from the ruins and debris of the mainland site. To do this he scraped away the rocks and threw them into the water. Sure enough, he left the old site a bare rock just as Ezekiel said.[6] Today fishermen really do spread their nets there to dry. Dad has been there and seen them.

More than three hundred prophecies were made in the Old Testament concerning the coming of a Messiah, which were literally fulfilled in the life of Jesus Christ. Since the Old Testament was translated into Greek around 250 B.C., the Hebrew Bible had to be completed before this time. Therefore, all the prophecies about the Messiah were written several hundred years before Christ actually showed up on earth.

The Old Testament predicted that Jesus would be born of a virgin (Isaiah 7:14). It predicted that He would be a descendant of Abraham (Genesis 12:1-3), from the tribe of Judah (Genesis 49:10), of the house of David (2 Samuel 7:12). It even pinpointed His birthplace as Bethlehem (Micah 5:2). It was prophesied that His ministry would be one of preaching (Isaiah 61:1-3) and healing (Isaiah 35:3-6), and that He would speak in parables (Psalm 78:2-4). His triumphal entry on a colt was foretold (Zechariah 9:9), as well as His betrayal for thirty pieces of silver (Zechariah

11:12-13). The facts that He would be abandoned by His disciples (Zechariah 13:6-7), then beaten and spit on (Isaiah 50:6), mocked (Psalm 22:7-8), that His hands and feet would be pierced (Psalm 22:16), that He would be crucified with criminals (Isaiah 53:12), offered gall mixed with vinegar to drink (Psalm 69:21), and have lots cast for His clothing (Psalm 22:18) were all Old Testament predictions. None of His bones were broken (Psalm 22:17), yet His side was pierced (Zechariah 12:10) just as the prophets forecast. Then He was buried with the wealthy (Isaiah 53:9).

It would have been humanly impossible for anyone to engineer a feat fulfilling even a quarter of these predictions — a fact which points not only to Jesus Christ as the true Messiah, but also to the Old Testament, written centuries before, as the inspired and reliable Word of God.

THE EVIDENCE OF MANUSCRIPT INTEGRITY

Many people mistakenly think that the Bible we have today is the end of a long succession of translations (Hebrew to Greek; Greek to Latin; Latin to German; German to English; English to whatever). They figure each one probably lost something in the translation, ruining the integrity of the text. You've played the "whisper game" before. By the time "I had a ham sandwich on white bread for lunch" is whispered from ear to ear more than five times it becomes totally distorted. It turns out something like "I have Arab sand, which John might rent for a bunch."

Well, this is not what took place with the Bible. The Old Testament was written in Hebrew, except for a little Aramaic, and the New Testament was written in Greek. The English Bibles we use today were translated directly from those original languages — not some intermediary one.

We do not have the original manuscripts for any of the books of the Bible. However, we do have a huge number of early copies of the originals. And the time span between the date the original was written and the date of the earliest copy we now have is extremely short. We have over 14,000 copies of early New Testament writings, with some of them having been copied less than one hundred years after the original was written.

Compare this with Plato's writings. The earliest manuscripts we have of his were copied 1,200 years after the original was written and there are only seven such manuscripts. Aristotle's works were written 1,400 years before the existing copies, and we have only five of these manuscripts.[7] Yet no one questions the fact that the books we now read really contain the actual words of Plato and Aristotle. (See what your English teacher says when you bring this up! On second thought, maybe that's not such a good idea.) Demosthenes, Euripedes, Sophocles, Thucydides, Caesar, and on and on — none of these writers' works are anywhere close to as accurately preserved as the words of our Bible, both Old and New Testaments.

The Jewish scribes who copied the biblical manuscripts went to extreme measures to be sure their copies were 100 percent accurate. They were meticulous in copying and counting each letter, word, and line. If a manuscript was off by just one letter, or a single mistake was discovered, the entire manuscript was burned. Scholars, who do this kind of stuff for a living, judge the copies we have of our New Testament to be 99.5 percent accurate — more accurate than any other ancient, widely accepted works of literature.[8] Critics who discard the Bible as an unproven manuscript, or as historically untrustworthy, refuse to apply the same standards to it that they do to other ancient writings.

THE EVIDENCE OF CHANGED LIVES

But it was men who chose which books to include in the Bible and which ones to discard, right? This is a question often posed by critics of the Bible. It is true that it wasn't until A.D. 393, at the Council of Hippo, and A.D. 397, at the Council of Carthage, that the New Testament text as a whole was solidified. But was it really up to these early church fathers to choose which books to leave in and which ones to take out? No, the criteria for selection were highly objective. The books had to be written or sanctioned by an apostle — one of the Twelve minus Judas, plus Paul — to whom Jesus had spoken directly, they had to be written during the first century and used by the early churches, and they had to be consistent with apostolic doctrine.[9] The men attending these councils didn't choose which books remained. They just observed. They noticed that God used certain books and not others in the lives of believers. The ones that met the criteria, and that God was obviously using to change hearts and lives, were put together in one unit called the Bible. So it was God, working in people's lives, who actually determined which books should be included.

Think about the process in our everyday lives. We have an old, 8-track tape player hidden away in our family room closet. I won't throw it away because one day it might be considered an antique. When I was a teenager, it was the hottest new thing to hit the shelves of the big, new department store in town. But it took only a few years for it to become obsolete. Newer and better tape players came along, then CD players, and soon 8-tracks were a thing of the past. Manufacturers stopped making them completely. Why? Because nobody bought them anymore. Why did they stop buying them? Because they no longer had any validity. They did nothing to help people in their daily lives. They didn't work nearly as well as the newer, more modern inventions.

Ah, but look at that safety pin — the one holding your backpack together. Do you know how long safety pins have been around? A long, long time. As a matter of fact, they were patented in 1849 by Walter Hunt of New York.[10] Why is a simple little invention like the safety pin still around after 150 years, while much more intricate inventions, like 8-track players, became passé in less than five years? Because safety pins continue to work and have validity in people's lives.

The Bible would be obsolete by now — invalid — if it didn't make a difference; if people's lives weren't continually changed by its message.

THE PROBLEM OF INTERPRETATION

So, suppose the Bible really is the inspired Word of God as it claims to be and the copies we have today are accurate accounts of what was originally written. We still have one more problem — the problem of interpretation. Doesn't every religious denomination interpret the message of the Bible differently?

Actually that is not the case. The fact is that most denominations agree on the foundational truths of the Bible — God, man, sin, and salvation. Most Christians will affirm the Apostles' Creed. When disagreements over interpretation occur, it is usually because inconsistent methods of interpretation are being used. Often people tend to apply their own preconceived ideas instead of letting Scripture speak for itself. Or they struggle over whether to interpret a passage literally (believing it word for word as it is written), or figuratively (accepting that figures of speech, word pictures, or prophecy are being used to make a point).

The truth is that in every case, the interpretation should be made "normally." Most problems of interpretation disappear when the reader asks himself one simple question: What did the original author want his original readers to understand in this situation? Was he writing poetry and therefore painting word pictures for his readers? Was he foretelling the future but trying to explain these future events in terms of present knowledge? Was he using allegories (stories and symbols) to get his point across? The author's original intent would be the "normal" interpretation. This makes context a crucial issue in interpretation. Taken out of context, verses can be twisted to mean many different things.

Take for example your opinion that doing homework is a big waste of time. Suppose you e-mailed a classmate tonight and wrote something like: "My English teacher gives us too much homework. Having to sit in my bedroom and write twenty vocabulary cards every night is a real pain in the neck. I would much rather be out playing basketball." Two hundred years from now if someone unearths your e-mail from within the bowels of an obsolete thing called a computer, he'll have to decide whether writing vocabulary cards (whatever they were) caused an actual physical malady affecting the neck area, or if you were merely trying to communicate a distaste for this particular exercise. Out of context, it would seem that vocabulary cards should be avoided at all costs or one's health might be in jeopardy. However, taking into account your original reader (a sixth-grade buddy) and checking out the other context clues in the text will no doubt lead the reader to the latter conclusion.

The same process is valid with biblical interpretation. The Bible contains poetry, prophecy, parables, visions, and historical narratives. To interpret a passage correctly, we must understand what type of literature we are dealing with, as well as the context. Factual description must be understood differently from figures of speech, historical narrative differently from Hebrew poetry. It is when we fail to examine the context and understand the type of literature being used that we run into problems of interpretation.

Here's an example. According to Isaiah 11:12, God will gather the scattered people of Judah "from the four corners of the earth" (KJV). This does not imply that Isaiah, inspired by God, really believed that the earth had four corners any more than the author of Leviticus believed that men had four corners on their heads ("Ye shall not round the corners of your heads," 19:27, KJV). This is picturesque language, used in much the same way as biblical writers used the terms "rising of the sun" or "going down of the same" (Psalm 113:3; 19:4-6). We know that the sun does not actually move across the sky, yet today we use similar picturesque or descriptive language ("sunrise" and "sunset") to convey this same phenomenon even in our highly sophisticated weather reports. Unfortunately, some of our early church leaders misinterpreted passages such as these and wound up assuming that the world was flat. They later tried Galileo as a heretic for teaching that the sun is the center of our solar system around which the planets rotate. But we cannot blame the Bible for the erroneous scientific conclusions made by clergymen. We, ourselves, must seek to be consistent and to remain true to the author's intent as we interpret and apply biblical truths to our lives, so that we can avoid making similar mistakes.

SUMMARY

Numerous attempts have been made over the centuries to burn, ban, and otherwise eliminate the Bible, but all have failed. Critics have continually tried to discredit it. Yet, there it sits on your desk. It has been copied, translated, and circulated more than any other book in history. The continual proof of its historical accuracy; its single, unified message in the midst of extreme diversity; the fulfillment of hundreds of prophecies; the reliability of the manuscripts; the fact that for over two millennia it has continued to change lives — these are all evidences the Bible is more, much more, than just a manmade document.

QUESTION #4

DID THE MIRACLES IN THE
Bible Really Happen?

A LITTLE WOODEN PREACHER-MAN WADDLED IN AND OUT OF A LITTLE wooden church whenever we wound the stem on the little wooden music box. The church doors opened and closed as the music played and the black-clad, little clergyman appeared and disappeared in rhythmic synchronization. The music and motion were magic to Jonathan's four-year-old ears and eyes. He sat mesmerized by their spell for long periods of time.

But one day he could not keep his stubby fingers off the music box any longer. He just had to peer inside to see where that little guy went and what made him come back out. As the doors were snapped off their hinges, the little man fell to the floor still attached to a long wire. That day Jonathan discovered gears and cogs, pulleys and wires. That day he destroyed the magic of motion. Even with a lot of glue and some rubber bands, my special music box never again worked the way it used to — but at least Jon-jon had gained some understanding of its inner mechanisms.

Jonathan was, and still is, a very pragmatic child. (Go look it up in the dictionary. It's a nice way of saying "nosy.") He wouldn't believe anything until he could touch and see it for himself. I recall a jack-in-the-box that popped its way right out of the box when he was just two! I guess that's why I'm not surprised that he is the one always wanting the lowdown on the Bible's miracles. What really happened? Did God actually stop rivers in midstream, swoop people up to heaven in chariots, walk on water, and heal a multitude of diseases?

If he could, Jonathan would take each miracle apart, just like he did that music box, and look inside. He would search for hidden "wires" that might be attached. He would try to discover the "cogs" and "wheels" that set each miracle in motion, so that he could have a rational explanation. But if miracles could be opened up and figured out, they would be destroyed — just like the music box. You see, miracles by their very nature have to remain unexplainable, unnatural, unsolved — or they aren't miracles. However, there are a few things that we *can* understand about miracles.

WHAT IS A MIRACLE?

In order to define a miracle we must first distinguish between wonders of nature and miracles. You've heard people refer to such things as the birth of a baby or the blooming of a flower as "miracles." Certainly these are marvelous events. They cause us to wonder at the awesome majesty and intricacy of God's handiwork. But they are natural events — happenings that occur in the normal course of life. To define them as miraculous is to dilute the concept of miracles and discredit the fact that miracles really do take place. Miracles are occurrences or events contrary to the nature of our three-dimensional universe. They are *un*natural actions that *super*sede the normal laws of science and nature. They take place in the realm of the *super*natural.

So what *is* a miracle? Here's an example I've heard before that really helps. Let's adapt it to our lives. Outside on the back deck we have a table. On that table is a basket of beautiful red and pink flowering impatiens (as long as I remember to water them!). Often we can find Storm, the stray cat Ben adopted, curled up next to that basket for a snooze in the sunshine. Let's say one of you is outside on a beautiful Saturday morning, sitting at that table drinking a Coke and reading the newspaper. Okay, so we're already well beyond the realm of reality here. We rarely have such quiet moments at our house, and seldom do any of you guys read the newspaper. But anyway, let's say it starts to get very warm in the Florida sunshine, and you and Storm both decide to head into the cooler shade of the porch. At this point the basket of flowers is astounded. "How did they do that?" it wonders as it wilts in the heat. "It must be a miracle!" And indeed it would be a miracle for a plant to get up and move itself into the shade. What is a natural act for you and the cat, as superior beings, would be a miracle for a plant to accomplish.

So now, you and the cat are sitting on the porch. You continue to read the paper. You mention out loud to nobody in particular, "Oh, dear. The paper says it's going to rain tomorrow afternoon. That's really going to mess up our picnic!" You get up and go inside to make some phone calls, leaving a crumpled newspaper and an astonished cat on the porch.

"How on earth did he do that?" the cat mutters as he walks all over the paper. He sniffs and he snorts, he scratches and he rolls, but try as he might he cannot decipher a thing about the next day's weather from that section of the paper. Sure enough, the next day it pours. "It's a miracle," the cat concludes, remembering your prediction from the previous day. And indeed it is — to the cat. For a cat to decipher anything from a newspaper would definitely be a *super*natural accomplishment. What is a natural act for you, as a superior being, would be a miracle for a cat to accomplish.

Can you see where I'm going with this? What is *un*natural for us as human beings living in a three-dimensional universe might actually be commonplace to a Superior Being. Neither the plant's inability to explain your movement into the shade, nor the cat's inability to explain your reading the newspaper nullifies that those events took place. The fact that we cannot explain miracles in no way invalidates them.

If there is indeed an all-powerful God who is not confined by space and time as we concluded in answering Question #1, and if He chooses to interact in our world, then miracles can certainly take place. What is a miracle to us, as inferior beings, would be commonplace to Him in all His superiority. David DeWitt, in *Beyond the Basics,* defines miracles as the "reasonable actions of a superior being."[1]

Here's another example, which might be even more helpful. It's found in Edwin Abbott's *Flatland,* first published in 1884. In his story, a three-dimensional spherical being chooses to show up in a two-dimensional flat land where only length and width are known. Height is meaningless. Several "miracles" appear to take place for the Flatlanders as this sphere enters their world. First, a Point appears out of nowhere on the horizon. It becomes a Circle and grows larger and larger. All of a sudden it stops growing and begins to shrink until it becomes a Point once again and disappears as incredibly as it appeared. The Flatlanders are abuzz trying to describe and explain this totally unnatural and unreasonable event. However, to the three-dimensional being, nothing out of the ordinary happened. His actions were totally in keeping with his nature as he passed through the Flatlanders' limited world.[2]

In the same way, if God is sovereign, and if He created a universe in which He controls all dimensions beyond the three in which we live, wouldn't it be reasonable for Him to choose to penetrate that universe? And if He did, wouldn't His presence cause what appear to be miraculous events — such as those described in the Bible?

Think about those 3-D ads that sometimes appear in magazines, or the 3-D films that come out at the movies every once in a while. They are impossible to decipher without the special glasses that are supposed to accompany them. They make no sense whatsoever. They're just a mumbo jumbo of odd shapes and color combinations. However, when you put the glasses on, they make wonderful sense. Butterflies appear to hover, as if waiting to land on your palm, and snowflakes seem like they will surely melt on your tongue if you stick it out.

In the same way, what is natural and beautiful to sovereign eyes makes no sense at all to human eyes with limited vision. To discount or disregard miracles is to restrict God — to *limit* Him. No, actually it's worse than that. It's to *eliminate* Him completely. If you rule out miracles, you rule out God and Christianity completely.

MIRACLES ARE ESSENTIAL TO CHRISTIANITY

You can do away with miracles in Islam or Confucianism. You can eradicate them from Taoism or Buddhism. You can even eliminate miracles completely from Hinduism where they are prominent. Even without miracles all these religions stay intact. Not so with Christianity. If you eliminate miracles, you have to eliminate Christianity completely as a world religion. Without miracles Christianity cannot stand. All of its most important, validating events involve miracles. The creation of the world, the ten plagues, the exodus of the nation of Israel from Egypt, and many of the conquests in the Promised Land all center around the occurrence of miracles. The virgin birth of Jesus was indeed a miracle. Jesus Christ Himself validated His own ministry and His claim to be the Messiah by performing miracles. (See Matthew 11:2-5; John 10:25; 14:11; 15:24.)

It is interesting that none of the witnesses to these miracles — even those hostile to Christ's teachings, like the Pharisees and Sadducees — ever *denied* that the miracles took place. They never challenged the miracles themselves. They only challenged the source of the power Jesus used to perform them (see Matthew 12:24) or His right to do them (see Matthew 21:23). If Jesus had actually walked on a sandbar instead of on the water, don't you think the disciples' story would have been challenged? If He had actually used available food to feed the five thousand or only cured psychosomatic disorders (illnesses that were all in people's minds), wouldn't His enemies have jumped on the chance to discredit Him? There is no record of anyone refuting the miracles Jesus did.

THE RESURRECTION — THE GREATEST MIRACLE OF ALL

What about the Resurrection? If the miracles recorded in the Bible did not really take place, then the resurrection of Jesus Christ, *the most crucial claim in all of Christianity*, never took place either. Christianity would be based entirely on a lie, albeit the most successful lie ever perpetrated in history. Millions of people over the centuries have based their lives on it, and millions have lost their lives because of it.

If this is indeed the case, then Christians should be the most pitied people who have ever lived and believed in anything. In

1 Corinthians 15:17-19, Paul tells us that without the Resurrection, our faith is useless. The actual Greek word he uses here is *kenos.* Literally translated it means "vain" or "empty." It is used to describe sewer water. The Christian faith without the Resurrection is as useless as filthy, dirty sewer water!

Who would have originated such a lie? Certainly not the enemies of Jesus. They wouldn't have wanted anyone to believe that He had really risen as He had prophesied He was going to. No, it could only have been originated by Jesus' followers. But why would they manufacture such a hoax?

Maybe they were so full of grief that they mistakenly looked in the wrong tomb. Finding it empty, they figured the Resurrection had occurred and spread the word. (Just like last week when I thought the car was stolen from the parking garage — but I was actually looking on the wrong level!) But if this were true, the enemies could have easily produced the body and dispelled the rumor immediately.

What if they were just hallucinating, hoping *SO* much that Jesus was alive that they really truly thought they saw Him? Well, that would mean that over a period of forty days more than five hundred people had the same hallucination. Yet, even by placing a thousand people in the same room, under the same stresses, using the same drugs, scientists would have a hard time getting two of them to have a similar hallucination.

Maybe the disciples purposely concocted a huge scheme to spread a story they knew was false, just so they could validate the ministry they had dedicated their lives to for the previous three years. If so, they were willing to be put in prison, whipped, beheaded, crucified, and fed to lions for a lie. They were willing to sacrifice their social status, their political power, and all their possessions. They wound up hated and scorned wherever they went to spread their tale.

Charles Colson wrote a book called *Loving God*. In a chapter titled "Watergate and the Resurrection" he discusses the Watergate break-in during Richard Nixon's presidency. You weren't alive then (not even close), but it was the cover-up of this illegal action that cost several of our highest-ranking government officials (including Colson) their jobs and a lot of jail time. President Nixon himself was forced to resign in disgrace. Although the break-in took place in June of 1972, the serious cover-up scheme began on March 21, 1973. It ended just a few days later on April 8, 1973. Colson says this about their attempt to fabricate and perpetuate a lie:

With the most powerful office in the world at stake, a small band of handpicked loyalists, no more than ten of us, could not hold a conspiracy together for more than two weeks . . . no one was in grave danger; no one's life was at stake. Yet after just a few weeks the natural human instinct for self-preservation was so overwhelming that the conspirators, one by one, deserted their leader, walked away from their cause, turned their backs on the power, prestige, and privileges.[3]

He continues, contrasting the scandal he and his fellow government officials took part in with the events that surrounded the resurrection of Jesus Christ:

The Watergate cover-up reveals, I think, the true nature of humanity. . . . Is it really likely, then, that a deliberate cover-up, a plot to perpetuate a lie about the Resurrection, could have survived the violent persecution of the apostles, the scrutiny of early church councils, the horrendous purge of the first-century believers who were cast by the thousands to the lions for refusing to renounce the Lordship of Christ? Is it not probable that at least one of the apostles would have renounced Christ before being beheaded or stoned? Is it not likely that some "smoking gun" document might have been produced exposing the "Passover plot"? Surely one of the conspirators would have made a deal with the authorities (government and Sanhedrin probably would have welcomed such a soul with open arms and pocketbooks!). . . . Take it from one who was inside the Watergate web looking out, who saw firsthand how vulnerable a cover-up is. Nothing less than a witness as awesome as the resurrected Christ could have caused those men to maintain to their dying whispers that Jesus is alive and Lord.[4]

Many people have set out to prove that the story of Christ's resurrection was nothing more than a myth. Frank Morison, an English journalist, was one of them. He wanted to dismiss the disciples' claims that Christ was alive. He wanted to find alternative reasons that would explain why the tomb was empty and the rock rolled away that first Easter morning. He wanted to investigate the fact that the authorities couldn't produce Jesus' body following the Crucifixion and the possibility that the disciples had stolen the body. He wanted to prove once for all to the world that Jesus did not rise from the dead.

However, the more he looked at the evidence, both scientifically and rationally, and the more he applied the same standards he did for other historical evidence, the more he became convinced that there was only one possible explanation: Jesus did indeed rise from the dead. The book he planned to write disproving the Resurrection became a book providing evidence that the

Resurrection really did occur. He titled it *Who Moved the Stone?*

Two young Englishmen, Lord Lyttleton and Gilbert West, attended Oxford in the eighteenth century. They were determined to attack the foundations of the Christian faith and discredit it completely. Lyttleton decided he would try to prove that Saul of Tarsus was never really converted to Christianity. West's task was to invalidate the resurrection of Jesus Christ.

When they met to discuss their findings, they were surprised to find that each of them had independently come to the same conclusion. Lyttleton concluded that Saul really had become a radically changed man as a result of his conversion to Christianity. West found that the evidence overwhelmingly pointed to the fact that Jesus had risen from the dead. Their findings were published in *Observations on the History and Evidences of the Resurrection of Jesus Christ* in 1747.[5]

Here's a book you've probably heard about and may have even read. I know you've watched the movie. General Lew Wallace wanted to create a historical novel about the events surrounding the death and supposed resurrection of Jesus. As he did research for his book, the historical evidence for the Resurrection became so powerful that he ended up writing *Ben-Hur* as a new believer.

C. S. Lewis had no intention of accepting Jesus as God's Son, but in his search for truth, as the evidence of the Resurrection unfolded before him, he describes himself as being brought "kicking and struggling" from the world of atheism into the kingdom of God.[6]

I, too, find it highly unlikely that eleven Jewish men would have invented such an incredible myth for no reason at all, and then been willing to suffer and die for it. That they then would be followed by millions of others over the course of two millennia makes the plausibility of discounting the Resurrection miracle even more remote. No one to date has been able to concoct a valid, *natural* scientific explanation for the historical facts related to the Resurrection.

If the Resurrection miracle *did* indeed take place, every other miracle in the Bible becomes plausible. If God could raise Jesus from the dead, what's a little manna from heaven? Or a few fish for lunch? Or a stroll through a raging riverbed suddenly gone dry? If God is truly God, is there anything He cannot do?

WHY MIRACLES OCCURRED

Did miracles occur as a means of causing people to believe? No! Often the opposite took place. Pharaoh saw the same miracles the Israelites did, yet his heart was hardened (see Exodus 9:34-35). The Pharisees observed a demon cast out, a blind man healed, a withered hand restored, even a dead man raised. The more miracles they saw, the more they plotted to get rid of Jesus (see John 11:47-53). No, the purpose of miracles was not to coerce people into belief. Miracles were God's way of authenticating that a message or a messenger was sent from Him (see Hebrews 2:3-4).

Miracles did not happen at equal intervals and in equal amounts all through biblical times. Most occurred at three specific times in history — the time of Moses, when the nation of Israel was leaving Egypt and entering the Promised Land; the time of Elijah and the prophets, as the nation was about to be dispersed and destroyed; and at the time of Christ and the apostles. Almost all of the miracles recorded in the Scriptures are clustered around these three brief periods when God was revealing and validating His Word as given in the Law via Moses, then by the prophets, and ultimately through the Messiah. They are separated by hundreds of years. But it's interesting to note that even during these three brief time periods when many miraculous events took place, most of the people on earth — even the most genuine believers — never witnessed any of them.

The fact that miracles do not seem to be prevalent today does not invalidate their occurrence. (You don't have to ever see a buffalo to believe that at one time they roamed our western plains in abundance, do you?) The question we have to answer isn't, "Do miracles occur now?" It's, "Could they have occurred back then?"

SCIENCE AND MIRACLES

The Greeks believed that Zeus manufactured lightning bolts and hurled them to the earth whenever he was ticked off. Then science proved that lightning was caused by electrical storms produced by atmospheric conditions. The Greeks also believed that the personality of the ocean was dependent on the mood of the god Poseidon. Once again science proved them wrong. Scientific findings do sometimes discount religious beliefs. However, science has never disproved the occurrence of miracles.

Science is a study designed to show us the way things usually work in nature. It formulates laws to express these findings. Miracles are exceptions to the laws of science. However, they presuppose that such laws exist. If there were no scientific laws, there would be no sense in calling anything a miracle.

It's important to remember that exceptions to a law do not disprove it. Right? Let me explain.

There is a beautiful mountain in North Carolina called Grandfather Mountain. You guys were very little when we visited there, but I'm sure you'll never forget it. The sheer rock cliff drops off thousands of feet to the valley below. I hate to even think about it, but what if one of you had slipped while we stood looking over the edge? (My knees get weak thinking about my four squirrelly little boys standing just a slippery footstep away from their deaths.)

The law of gravity demands that if that had happened you would have fallen down, down, down, all the way to the bottom of the canyon.

But what if you were attached to a hang glider? Wind currents in that canyon might even *lift* you so that you could land on a higher ledge. Do the principles of aerodynamics nullify the law of gravity? No, in this case they just supersede it.

In a miracle, a higher principle (a *super*natural law) is superseding a lower principle (a natural or scientific law). God instituted what we call laws of nature, but He is not bound by them. He can choose to supersede them in order to reveal Himself or verify His message.

Here's another example. Suppose one of you went to work for Dr. Tom at his veterinary clinic this Christmas during your vacation. Let's say he promises you $200 if you come in each morning for those two weeks and walk the dogs boarded in the kennels. So you sign a contract with him for that amount. However, when you go to pick up your paycheck at the end of the two weeks, you find that it is made out for $225. Did Dr. Tom nullify the original contract by giving you the extra $25? No! He just added to it. He gave you a bonus. In the same way, miracles do not violate the laws of science and nature. They just add to them.

Often people try to explain away the miracles. They try to make everyday scientific laws apply to them. Take, for instance, the crossing of the Red Sea in the book of Exodus. They try to explain that the extremely strong wind mentioned in the biblical account actually held the water back, not letting it flow down the riverbed. This allowed the Israelites to cross on dry land with water being pushed back on one side. Well, according to Exodus 14:21-22, God *did* raise up a very strong wind. This wind piled the water up in great walls on *both* sides of their path, upstream and downstream, drying the land for them to walk between. Either way, the wind still seems like a miraculous one to me!

Can you imagine getting three million men, women, and children plus their carts and cattle across a riverbed, which at some points was as wide as the state of Florida, while the wind held the water back the whole time? It actually could have taken days for the whole nation of people and their belongings to cross. A wind strong enough to hold back the water, and sustained long enough to allow all those people to cross, is definitely outside the boundaries of natural science. It is a miracle!

Some people insist that the crossing of the Red Sea probably took place during a dry spell, or at a place where the water was not very deep to begin with, or at the shallow Reed Sea, which was incorrectly recorded as the Red Sea. They insist that the people could have actually just waded across. Wow! That's even more miraculous — to think that Pharaoh's entire army, including all his horses and chariots, was drowned in a trickling stream! (They must have been wearing extremely heavy armor!)

SUMMARY

I challenge you all, especially Jonathan, to go ahead and investigate the miracles for yourself. Try to take them apart. Trust me, you will never understand the workings of all the "cogs" and "wheels" and all the "pulleys" and "wires." That's because miracles are *super*natural, beyond our limited understanding. But an honest investigation of God's supernatural actions can only lead you into a deeper understanding of Him.

The word *miracle* means "sign" in New Testament Greek, and that is exactly what the miracles are. They are signs that point beyond — to something beyond our natural world, past the scientific laws we have established to explain it. They reveal the *super*natural. They reveal God to us, and they validate the messengers He sends to proclaim His Word.

Miracles are essential to Christianity. Without miracles Christianity is totally invalid. Without the Resurrection, Christians are complete fools. The bottom line is this: If God exists, then miracles are possible. And if the miracles of the Bible really did happen, and Christ really did rise from the dead, He has to be more, *much* more than just a great human being around whom all of history is dated. He has to be the Son of God — just as He claimed. We'll look at this more as we deal with Question #5.

QUESTION #5

Isn't It Narrow-Minded to *Say That Jesus Is the Only Way to God?*

This question has become a huge stumbling block for your generation. The need for *open*-minded tolerance of everything and everyone has been strongly emphasized throughout much of your education. You have been taught that you must not only accept differences in others, but you must embrace them as well — especially when it comes to religious beliefs. If you don't, you are considered *narrow*-minded — and to be labeled *narrow*-minded in our society is socially unacceptable.

I totally agree that tolerance is a virtue that must be taught and acquired in order for a society to survive. But there is a flip side to the tolerance issue that seldom comes up. In fact, in some areas and facets of life open-mindedness is not acceptable at all. Sometimes *intolerance* is not only good — it is vital. Let me give you some examples.

The Department of Transportation (DOT) has just opened a crosstown toll road near our house. It is designed to ease congestion within the city limits and help get folks in and out of town in a hurry. However, there is one point about its construction that I would like to argue with the DOT. The westbound on-ramp is a real pain to use. First of all, you have to turn left off a busy street to enter it, which often takes two cycles of the traffic light. Then you have to travel about a quarter mile in the opposite direction before the ramp heads back toward the highway. By the time you wind your way back to the parkway, pay your toll, and accelerate into the flow of traffic, you feel like you've wasted most of the time you were supposed to save by using the parkway.

There has to be a better way. But for some reason, the DOT, knowing a whole lot more about the situation than we do, decided that this was the best alternative. It could be argued that they are being very narrow-minded about the whole situation. Often, in my haste, I think about how much quicker and easier it would be if I veered right before I got to the traffic light, headed up the sloping bank alongside the highway, found a gap in the guardrail, and just drove out onto the asphalt road. That way I could avoid the traffic light, ignore the toll, and be spared a whole lot of inconvenience. However, if I did that I would probably get a ticket (since their narrow-mindedness causes them to be very intolerant). More than likely I would get stuck in the mud on the bank. Or there is a possibility that I would be hit broadside by a speeding truck as I entered without benefit of a merge lane.

I have to face it. No matter how much I might choose to disagree, there is only one way to get onto the parkway — the way the DOT intended for me to get there.

Is it wrong for the DOT to be narrow-minded about the use of its on- and off-ramps? Why not just let everyone get on the toll road any way they choose, whatever way seems best at the time?

That really sounds ridiculous, doesn't it? All kinds of accidents would occur; the private property bordering the highway would be damaged; no tolls would be collected to pay for repairs; and so on. No, for our sakes, the DOT has to be narrow-minded and therefore intolerant of any deviance from their plans.

NARROWNESS DOES NOT MAKE SOMETHING WRONG

The point I am trying to make is that just because something is narrow does not automatically make it wrong. Narrowness can be very good. You have to admit that you want a narrow-minded pilot in the cockpit when you're about to board a plane. You don't want a pilot who will land on runway 6A from the north when he's supposed to come in on runway 6A from the south. You want him to be intolerant of any deviation from the control tower's orders.

A narrow-minded pediatrician insists on giving immunizations to babies no matter how much they fuss in order to ensure their health and well-being later in life. A narrow-minded policeman will not tolerate drunk driving in his efforts to keep our streets safe. No, just because something is narrow-minded does not imply that it is wrong.

TRUTH IS ALWAYS NARROW

The fact of the matter is that *all "truth" is narrow*. In order to be defined as "truth," a body of knowledge has to be absolutely intolerant of error. Take mathematics for example. Math is a very narrow subject. One plus one equals two. This is a mathematical truth — and a very narrow one. There is no way you can convince any of your math teachers that this is not so. If you do not accept this one, very basic, very narrow truth, you will not pass a single math exam following the first grade. How intolerant!

All the scientific laws (truths) that govern our universe are narrow. As much as we might wish it were not true, gravity will always cause us to fall to the ground if we slip from a tree branch, and centrifugal force will always pull us off the road if we travel around a curve too quickly.

SOCIETY DOES NOT DETERMINE TRUTH

Another important point we need to understand is that truth is not subject to society's whims and wishes. We've already talked about the fact (in answering Question #3) that for centuries, popular opinion determined the earth was flat. It didn't matter that just about everyone on the planet held to that belief — it was completely false. Scientific advances soon proved the earth was spherical. At first this was a very unpopular notion in society. People lost their lives trying to uphold it. Nonetheless, it was true. The determination of what is true has to be based on objective evidence, not subjective belief — no matter how many people hold to that belief.

SINCERITY DOES NOT DETERMINE TRUTH

This brings us to another prevalent misconception in our society. It is our tendency to want to believe that "sincerity makes it so." Sincerity is admirable, and it is much applauded in our society, but it has absolutely nothing to do with determining truth. I can recall many incidents from your life experiences that illustrate this. Remember the time that Zach sincerely believed that the side of his little tent would have a great trampoline effect if he ran and jumped against it at top speed? However, he was sincerely wrong and ripped the thing to shreds on his first attempt.

And do you remember Mr. Hubbard telling us about the time he drank bleach instead of lemonade? He had just finished mowing his yard on a hot Florida summer afternoon, and he went inside to get a drink. Unbeknownst to him, his wife had decided to bleach out the lemonade pitcher, which had become quite stained. There it sat on the counter filled to the brim with what he thought was lemonade. He poured a big glassful and took a swig. It only took a second for him to realize how wrong he was. He grabbed for the milk, only to find the bottle was empty. He ended up rushing to the grocery store and chugging a gallon of milk in the dairy aisle. Fortunately he was fine, and now he has a funny story to tell, which points out the invalidity of sincerity. He sincerely thought that the pitcher on the counter was full of refreshing lemonade. Not so!

Probably my most vivid memory of sincerity gone awry occurred when Matthew was tiny, maybe four years old. He came to me and asked if he could have a Superman cape. I found an old towel, cut it, and fastened it around his shoulders. Off he zoomed, running around and around the house, jumping off beds, chairs, couches — anything he could climb onto — with his cape flapping behind him. When he decided to leap from the table onto the kitchen countertop, across the sink and up onto the refrigerator, I figured it was time for him to head outdoors.

I watched through the window. Over and over MattE ran at top speed and flung himself into the air across an embankment that separated our house from the neighbor's. Over and over he leaped with his arms outstretched and kicked his feet out behind him. Over and over he landed smack on his belly and took a huge bite out of the neighbor's sod. Every time he would dust himself off, rearrange his cape and try again, sincerely expecting to take flight. I cringed each time he landed, but he didn't really seem to be in great danger of breaking any bones or dislodging any teeth. I figured that before long he would tire of the futile attempts and come back inside with a little less energy to spare.

When I next glanced out the window, my attention was drawn to a bright blue blob at the very top of the highest orange tree in our side yard. It was Matthew, poised and ready for a leap of true Superman proportions. I flung open the window and yelled, "MattE, NO! Don't jump. You'll kill yourself!" I ran outside and used every adult psychological technique I could think of to coax him down from his precarious perch. Finally I resorted to bribery and the promise of milk and cookies. I removed the cape and hid it while he had his snack.

You see, MattE was extremely sincere in his belief that the cape we had made would allow him to fly — so sincere that he was willing to sacrifice his life and limbs. But he was sincerely wrong. No matter how fast he ran or how high he climbed, he could never have taken flight. All the sincerity in the world wouldn't have helped.

There are many cases each year of a parent or sibling cleaning a gun he or she sincerely believes to be unloaded. But the gun goes off in the cleaning process and someone in the family is injured or killed. The person cleaning the gun was no doubt 100 percent sincere in the belief that the chamber was empty, but he or she was sincerely wrong.

Sincerity cannot change reality. You can believe something with all your heart, but if the object of that belief is not valid, the sincerity does absolutely no good. All the sincerity in the world will not turn bleach into lemonade; or help a little boy fly; or protect a person from a speeding bullet. Truth must be determined apart from sincerity.

CHRISTIANITY IS NARROW

So how does Christianity fit into all this? Those who believe that there really is a sovereign God who rules the universe (Question #1), and that the Bible is His inspired message (Question #3), must also conclude that Jesus Christ provides the *only* access to a relationship with Him. This is a very narrow belief. But narrowness is not the issue here. Truth is. Based on what the Bible says, this is the only conclusion that can be reached. Let me show you why.

If you ask your friends and teachers who they believe Jesus to be, many of them will say that He was a good man, or a wise leader, or perhaps a great moral teacher. Unfortunately none of these answers is valid. You see, Jesus made a very important claim. Unlike all other religious leaders — unlike Moses, Mohammed, Buddha, and Gandhi; unlike Confucius or Zoroaster or Joseph Smith — Jesus did not claim to be one among many who raised Himself up to the level of God. He claimed to be *the* one and only God who lowered Himself to our level to show us how we could have a relationship with God.

You've probably heard the modern parable about a farmer who finds an anthill in the path of his plow. He does not want to destroy the ants, and he struggles to find a way to communicate to them that they must move or be destroyed. He finally concludes that the only way he could ever possibly get this message across would be to become an ant himself and communicate the message to them on their own level. This illustrates exactly what Jesus did as Paul tells us in Philippians 2:6-8. As God, He lowered Himself in human form to our level. Living with us as a human being, He could then communicate in a form we could understand.

Jesus made it very clear that He claimed to *be* God. He said, "I and the Father are one" (John 10:30); "Anyone who has seen me has seen the Father" (John 14:9). He also made it very clear that He is the *only way to God*: "I am the way and the truth and the life. No one comes to the Father except through me" (John 14:6).

So you see, anyone who claims that Jesus was merely a good man, a wise leader, or a great moral teacher is wrong. Those are the very things He could not possibly have been. Jesus claimed to be the only way to God. If He knew He wasn't, then He was a liar, and not a good man at all. We should therefore not accept any of His teachings, and no one should have ever trusted His leadership. And if He claimed to be God — really believing that He was God — but He was mistaken, then He was crazy and His teachings are nothing but the ramblings of a madman. We put people like that in mental hospitals.

Some people try to claim that Jesus was a great prophet. Well, none of the other prophets ever claimed to be God. Jesus did. If His claim to be God was wrong, that would have made Him a very poor prophet. He would have been a false prophet, a blasphemer, a liar, and the Jewish leaders would have been right to demand that He be put to death by their laws. If Jesus' claim to be God, and the only one through whom we may have access to God, was correct, then He was more, much more, than a prophet. He was God in human form just as He claimed to be.

We are left with only three options. (1) Jesus was a liar claiming to be God but knowing He was not; or (2) He was a lunatic incorrectly believing He was God but falling far short; or (3) He was who He claimed to be — the God and the Lord of all creation. C. S. Lewis, a professor at Cambridge University and a former agnostic, put it this way when he presented this argument:

> I am trying here to prevent anyone saying the really fool-
> ish thing that people often say about him: "I'm ready to
> accept Jesus as a great moral teacher, but I don't
> accept his claim to be God." That is the one thing we
> must not say. A man who was merely a man and said

the sort of things Jesus said would not be a great moral teacher. He would either be a lunatic — on the level with the man who says he is a poached egg — or else he would be the Devil of Hell. You must make your choice. Either this man was, and is, the son of God; or else a madman or something worse.

He adds:

You can shut him up for a fool, you can spit at him and kill him as a demon; or you can fall at his feet and call him Lord and God. But let us not come up with any patronizing nonsense about his being a great human teacher. He has not left that open to us. He did not intend to.[1]

Jesus made a very narrow, very exclusive claim. He claimed to be God and to provide the only way to heaven. This message was at the heart of everything He did and said while He was here on earth. His disciples and early followers understood this. (Read Acts 4:8-12; Romans 6:23; Titus 2:13.) What's more convincing is that His critics understood this as well. They knew exactly who Jesus claimed to be. That's why they accused Him of blasphemy (Mark 2:6-7; John 10:30-33). That's why they nailed Him to a cross (Mark 14:61-64; John 5:18).

SO WHAT ABOUT THE OTHER WORLD RELIGIONS?

Christianity is not unique in its narrowness. All world religions claim to be exclusively right. Mohammed, Buddha, and Krishna all claimed to understand and hold *the* way to God. Even Hinduism, which seems to allow for different paths to nirvana, stresses the superiority of its own. They all make mutually exclusive claims. Either one is true and every other religion is false, or all are false. Logically they cannot all be true. This is called the Law of Non-contradiction. Anyone who claims that all religions are just different paths up the same mountain is completely mistaken. Each of their claims excludes this possibility.

The uniqueness in Christianity is in Jesus' claim to *be* God — not just to provide the way *to* God. All other world religions seek salvation through human effort. The type of effort is different for each one. But Christianity says that all of man's efforts are futile — salvation can only be provided by God.

The Bible teaches that we are sinful and therefore separated from God. Christ taught that the only way to bridge that gap is through acceptance of God's payment for sin — His own death on the cross as our substitute. He taught that we cannot bridge the gap on our own merit or with any amount of effort or any number of good deeds. We will discuss this in more depth when we get to Question #7.

If you accept that there is a God (Question #1) and that the Bible is a reliable source through which He relays His message to us (Question #3), then you must also accept Christ's narrow, exclusive claim to be the only way to God.

TRUTH IS UNIVERSAL

If Jesus' claims are true for me, they must also be true for you and for everyone else — no matter who they are, where they live, or what they now believe. Truth is universal. It applies to everyone everywhere.

Let me ask you something. What would have happened in our society if the scientists who discovered the polio vaccine had refused to share its universal value with the rest of the world? What if they had been afraid of being ridiculed or labeled intolerant if they insisted that everyone had to be immunized whether or not they understood or agreed with the vaccine's medical significance? Should they have kept it just for themselves and those who chose to be vaccinated? That would have been the tolerant thing to do. Fortunately it became a law that all children had to be vaccinated before entering school, and a worldwide polio epidemic was virtually eradicated. That was the loving thing to do. Tolerance when dealing with personal opinions is great, but tolerance when dealing with facts (truth) can be devastating.

Yet, often we are so afraid of being labeled "intolerant" or "unloving" by our society that we fail to share the "truth" we have discovered with those around us. We are afraid that someone will mistake our motives and confuse our message of love with one of exclusivity or superiority. Granted, some people are arrogant with the truth, but as D. T. Niles of Ceylon put it, Christianity is really just "one beggar telling another beggar where to find food."[2]

A little known Old Testament story perfectly illustrates this point. It's found in 2 Kings 7:3-20. The city of Samaria was under siege by the Arameans, and the occupants were dying of starvation. Four lepers were among those about to die. They were outcasts and no one had even crumbs left to throw to them. They decided to go to the Aramean camp and take their chances at surrendering. They figured the worst that could happen was death — which they were facing anyway.

When they got to the camp, they found it deserted. Earlier the Arameans had panicked, thinking they were about to be attacked by the Hittites and the Egyptians, and had abandoned camp in a big hurry. So when the lepers arrived, everything they could have ever wished for was theirs for the taking — food, drink, silver, gold, clothing. They grabbed everything they could possibly haul away and hid it. Load after load, tent after tent, they scrounged and hid.

Suddenly they had a change of heart. "We're not doing right," they admitted. "This is a day of good news and we are keeping it to ourselves" (verse 9).

They left everything behind and ran back to Samaria and reported the great news to the gatekeepers, who told the king. There was enough food for everyone, and they all lived happily ever after — or something like that.

The point is, if we have truly discovered a truth, we should not keep it to ourselves. Sure, others may misunderstand and disagree. (This happened in the leper story too. I didn't have time to tell the whole thing.) But it is wrong of us to keep truth to ourselves. We should not let labels and accusations keep us from sharing it. The same Christ who claimed He was God and the only way to heaven gave us a great commission. He told us to take the good news to the ends of the earth (see Matthew 28:19-20; Mark 16:15; Acts 1:8). It is definitely "good news"! We must not keep it to ourselves.

SUMMARY

Jesus Christ claims to *be* God and to provide the *only* access to God. These claims are very narrow. The question isn't whether or not Christianity is narrow. All world religions are narrow. The question is whether or not it is true. Remember, truth cannot be influenced by the passions of society or by personal sincerity.

Based on the claims of Jesus Christ, every individual must make a decision. Was Jesus an evil liar, whose teachings have tricked and taunted mankind for generations? Was He a raving

madman whose followers risked their lives to defend His luna-
cies? Or was He who He claimed to be, the Lord of all creation
and the only way to God? There are no other choices.

It is far more important to be considered *right*-minded by
God than to be considered *open*-minded by society.

QUESTION #6

WHAT ABOUT THOSE WHO
Have Never Heard About Jesus?

IN THE LAST CHAPTER WE TALKED ABOUT TRUTH BEING UNIVERSAL. IF SOME-
thing is true, it is true for everyone, everywhere, all the time. If
Jesus is the only way to heaven (as He claimed to be) and the only
One through whom we can have a relationship with God, then no
one, anywhere, at any time can come to God by any other means.
If this is true, then ignorance is no excuse. Claiming lack of knowl-
edge as a valid reason for not responding to the claims of Jesus
Christ just doesn't cut it!

Wow! I'll bet your head is reeling right now! You're thinking
things like: "Do you mean God is willing to send people to hell
even if no one got around to sharing the message of Jesus' life and
death with them? How can you worship such a mean, vindictive
God? What about the people who live in remote villages that no
missionaries have ever visited? Or how about primitive people
who have never seen a Bible? There are millions of people who
can't read for themselves. Aren't there still places on our planet

where the Bible hasn't been translated into the native language? So even if the natives *could* read, they would have no source of information. That doesn't seem fair or loving at all!"

I agree. It doesn't seem fair or loving at all. If God relied only on human beings to communicate His message of eternal life and death to the world, a whole lot of people would be in a heap of trouble. But there is a lot more to God's plan than what we humans are able to convey to each other. Let's talk about it.

One drizzly Saturday morning all four of you decided to go fishing off our neighbor's dock. Zach ran into the house to grab some bread so you could catch little shiners. (Those poor silvery fish were such easy prey for your tiny, breaded hooks!) Anyway, we were expecting company that evening. I had just started to clean the kitchen floor, since mud had been tracked all over the tile from previous excursions back and forth from the lake.

"Zach" — I caught him just as he was going out the back door with his bait — "I'm going to mop the kitchen floor, then I've gotta run to the grocery store. Tell the other guys NOT to come into the kitchen. I don't want ANYONE walking across this floor till I get home. You got that?"

"Yeah, uh-huh, sure, Mom," he replied, and bolted off toward the lake.

I closed the door behind him, put all the chairs on top of the table — like they do when they clean the school cafeteria — swept up as much dirt as I could, then mopped the floor. I was in a hurry to get to the store, so I left the mop in the bucket by the back door and the chairs on top of the table. I called our neighbor to ask her to keep an eye on you and ran to the store.

When I got back from the grocery store about forty-five minutes later, I was totally dismayed! Muddy footprints led from the back door, which was now wide open, to the refrigerator, all around the kitchen table (with the chairs still on top of it), and back out the door. It didn't take my emotions long to pass the "dismayed" stage. Soon I was very upset! You probably remember it well.

"Guys, get in here right away!" I hollered out the back door, bringing everyone except Zach scurrying to the porch. (He had left his brothers and gone to the neighbor's house to check out their new slingshots.)

"Okay, what's going on? How come you all disobeyed me and tromped through the kitchen when you weren't supposed to?" I demanded.

I received nothing but blank stares in response, so I went into a tirade about not listening or caring, disrespecting my wishes, and on and on.

"We didn't know," one of you finally argued. "Zach never told us."

Boy, was he in trouble! But I wasn't finished with the rest of you yet. I didn't completely buy your plea of ignorance.

"Just look around." I begged in frustration, gesturing at the room. "How could you not realize that I had just mopped the floor? Couldn't you see the bucket and the mop by the door? How about the chairs on the table? Is that where I normally put the chairs? And what about the fact that the tile actually looks clean for once?"

Sensing my disappointment and exasperation one of you finally admitted, "You're right, Mom. We could see that the floor was clean even though Zach never told us, but we really wanted some Kool-Aid."

Zach had not carried out his part of the deal. He had failed to deliver my message to you. But regardless, ignorance was not an acceptable excuse. The content of my message was obvious by the evidence I had left around. Yet you chose to ignore it. Needless to say, you spent the next half hour mopping the kitchen floor instead of catching fish!

God is a loving and caring God. Fortunately He does not leave matters of eternal life and death solely in the hands of those who have been privileged with knowledge. He is far more loving and intelligent than that! He has provided two additional ways for every human being who has ever stepped foot on this planet to become aware of the message of salvation apart from human intervention. Just as in the floor-washing incident, ignorance cannot be claimed as an excuse — because ignorance does not exist! Let's look at God's two provisions.

NATURAL REVELATION: NO ONE IS IGNORANT OF GOD'S EXISTENCE

Jonathan, if I walked into your room right now, I could tell an awful lot about you even if I had never met you. I would know that a very distinct person with a defined personality lives in that messy place. I would know that you love sports and collecting hubcaps; that your desk doesn't get much studying done on it (it's far too messy), that you mostly wear casual clothes, and that you have very big feet! I would know what kind of music you like from checking out the CD cases on the floor, and that you have some artistic abilities by the way you have arranged various posters and paraphernalia on your walls. I might even be able to tell what you did last night. If I checked through the pockets of the jeans sprawled across the floor, I could possibly find a movie ticket stub or a receipt from the ice cream shop at the mall. If I knew nothing at all about you, I would still be able to make a pretty good guess as to where you might be at that particular moment based on what I found and observed in the room. Policemen and investigators make a living doing this kind of thing.

In the first chapter of Romans, verse 20, the apostle Paul tells us that God has left enough stuff lying around in His creation that we can know a lot about Him even if no one else ever tells us a single thing. If we take the time to look around and investigate, we can understand that God is powerful, that He is divine, and we can even deduce that He is eternal. Let me go ahead and quote the verse in Romans for you:

For since the creation of the world God's invisible qualities — his eternal power and divine nature — have been clearly seen, being understood from what has been made, *so that men are without excuse* (emphasis mine).

The first four verses in Psalm 19 say:

The heavens declare the glory of God;
the skies proclaim the work of his hands.
Day after day they pour forth speech;
night after night they display knowledge.
There is no speech or language
where their voice is not heard.
Their voice goes out into all the earth,
their words to the ends of the world.

The Bible tells us that we cannot claim ignorance of God's existence. We are completely without excuse based on what we see, hear, taste, smell, and touch in the world around us. The birth of a baby, the opening of a flower, the force of a hurricane, the beating of a heart, the digestion of food, the constancy of the seasons, the love of a parent — all these point to a Supreme Being.

From our observations we can learn much more beyond just

the fact that a Supreme Being exists. We can understand a lot about this Supreme Being's character. We can know that He is organized and systematic. We can realize that He cares about minute details as well as great big ones. We can understand that He is awesomely powerful and incredibly artistic. We can figure that He loves variety and texture and color. (His favorite colors appear to be blue and green!) Above all else, we can be absolutely certain that He is superior to us. The vastness and the unfathomable scientific treasures of the oceans, the seasons and the tides, and the anatomy of the human body all point to an immensely Supreme Being.

Even Dr. Francis Crick, Nobel Prize winner for his mapping of DNA and a staunch atheist, acknowledges that all that we are and all that we have could not have been a matter of chance. It had to have been caused (just like we talked about in answering Question #1). Crick admits that the planet we live on could not possibly have existed long enough for DNA to have evolved into the form it now has. He acknowledges that there had to be a Superior Source. However in his 1981 book called *Life Itself,* he unfortunately (and almost hilariously) attributes the existence of DNA to superior alien beings who planted already existing DNA seeds on our planet nine billion years ago.[1] People are sometimes willing to get awfully far off base to try to explain away the existence of God!

Remember world-famous astronomer Dr. Allan Sandage, to whom I referred back in Question #1? His scientific observations led him to a very different conclusion — and ultimately to a belief in the God of the Bible as the source of all life.

No one — especially Dr. Crick! — can claim ignorance of an eternal, omnipotent creator. And every person is responsible for reacting to the knowledge he or she has received from God's universe. Yes, God has made Himself obvious through His creation.

QUESTION 6

INTERNAL MORAL STANDARDS (CONSCIENCE): NO ONE IS IGNORANT OF HIS OWN SIN

Each one of us also has an internal standard of goodness, known as our conscience. Whether it is the rituals of pagan worship, the Five Pillars of Islam, the Noble Eightfold Path or the Five Precepts of Buddhism, the Puja and Dharma of Hinduism, the Ten Commandments of Judaism and Christianity, or the neighborly good deeds of a person who calls himself an atheist, we all set standards for our own behavior and moral goodness. But here's the problem — not one of us is able to live completely up to the standards we set for ourselves, whatever they may be! In Romans 2:14-15, Paul puts it this way:

> Indeed, when Gentiles (non-Jewish people), who do not have the law (the Ten Commandments), do by nature things required by the law, they are a law for themselves, even though they do not have the law, since they show that the requirements of the law are written on their hearts, their consciences also bearing witness, and their thoughts now accusing, now even defending them.

We know that we do not live up to the standards we set for ourselves, and we know that this is wrong. Our consciences continually convict and accuse us.

Ecclesiastes 3:11 says that God has "set eternity in the hearts of men." There is an inborn knowledge that there is more, much more, to life than what we experience here on earth. As humans we have devised various religions in our egotistical search to try to accomplish "ultimate good" on our own. But regardless of the

WHAT ABOUT THOSE WHO HAVE NEVER HEARD ABOUT JESUS?

89

standard we choose as a moral measure of true goodness or righteousness, we always fall short.

The great Hindu leader and teacher Mahatma Gandhi lived one of the most outwardly moral lives of any human being. His existence was spent trying to attain perfection and trying to reach the standards he had set for moral purity. Yet, for all his devotion to his religion, just before his death he wrote in the introduction to his autobiography,

> For it is an unbroken torture to me that I am still so far from Him, Who as I fully know, governs every breath of my life, and Whose offspring I am. I know that it is the evil passions within that keep me so far from Him, and yet I cannot get away from them.[2]

The difference between the way we know we *ought* to live and the way we *actually* live is called sin in the Bible. Since we all know that we cannot live up to our *own* standards — let alone God's — there is not a single person who can claim ignorance of sin. So what are we going to do?

MAN'S OBLIGATION: RESPOND TO THE KNOWLEDGE HE HAS RECEIVED

Everyone has the option of seeking a relationship with the Superior, Eternal Being they know to exist — or of choosing to ignore the evidence of His existence. A choice must be made. And here's the best part! God has obligated Himself to respond to individuals who respond to His revelation — who want a relationship with the Master of the universe whom they know they cannot please on their own.

GOD'S OBLIGATION: REVEAL HIMSELF TO THOSE WHO SEEK THE MESSAGE OF JESUS CHRIST

Hebrews 11:6 tells us that "without faith it is impossible to please God, because anyone who comes to him must believe that he exists and that *he rewards those who earnestly seek him*" (emphasis mine).

God has promised that He will reveal Himself to those people who want to know Him and who admit that they are incapable of reaching Him on their own. When someone observes nature and realizes that there is a Superior Being who must have brought this all into existence; and when that same person, guided by his own conscience, realizes that there must be a Source of Goodness outside of himself from whom he is separated; and if that person cries out for help; God promises that He will bring someone or something into that person's life to present him with the message of how he can have a relationship with the Creator God of the universe.

In Jeremiah 29:13 God says, "You will seek me and find me when you seek me with all your heart," and 1 Chronicles 28:9 says, "The LORD searches every heart and understands every motive behind the thoughts. If you seek him, he will be found by you; but if you forsake him, he will reject you forever."

God has promised that those who respond positively to the evidence they have been given (God's existence and their own sin) will be provided with the knowledge that leads to salvation. Those who suppress it or reject it will remain separated from God.

The Bible gives us many examples of people who responded positively to the revelation they had been given and cried out for help. God always came through, revealing to them how they could have a relationship with Him.

The story of Rahab, the harlot, is found in Joshua 2:1-21. She had never been introduced to the God of the Israelites, yet just by observing the powerful things He had done for that nation, she realized that He existed. She realized that she didn't live up to *anyone's* standards of moral perfection (she was a prostitute!) and that based on her own efforts, she could never please the God who had been revealed to her nor could she have a relationship with Him. But she wanted to. So God sent two Israelite spies into her town (Jericho) and into her home. Based on her faith and obedience to the message of the spies, she and her family were the only ones saved when the whole city was destroyed (see Hebrews 11:31). She even became the great-great-grandmother of King David and an ancestor of Jesus Christ (see Matthew 1:5)!

Naaman the Syrian was healed of leprosy when he listened to a little Jewish slave girl who had obviously been sent to his household to tell him about the God he was seeking (see 2 Kings 5:1-19). Philip was miraculously sent to share the gospel message with an Ethiopian eunuch who wanted to know God (see Acts 8:26-40). A man named Cornelius was also seeking a relationship with the one true God. Peter was sent to him with the message of Jesus, and Cornelius became the first Gentile convert following Christ's resurrection (see Acts 10). (Christianity had been primarily a Jewish belief up until that time.)

Missionary records are full of stories about people who had been totally isolated from any message of the Bible, yet were seeking a God that they realized must exist based on what they saw around them and what was revealed to them through their own consciences. They realized that their own rituals and practices left them unfulfilled and separated from the God they wanted to know. Over and over God has responded to such longings by sending missionaries to tell them the story of Jesus Christ.

Granny and Bupah used to tell the story of the missionaries who were stationed at Tiffi, in Nigeria, West Africa before they arrived. These missionaries were the first white people to ever set foot in that part of the world. However, when they arrived, they were greeted lavishly and asked immediately if they had brought a black book with them. "We have been seeking God," the village chief informed them. "I have had a dream that a white man would arrive with a black book and tell us how we can know Him." The people in the village responded to the information that God had revealed to them, and God fulfilled their desire to know Him by sending a missionary.

A dentist friend of ours tells an even more dramatic story. A few years ago he went on a short-term missionary trip to the Amazon. As his team traveled farther and farther up the Amazon River, they noticed that the villages and tribes became more and more primitive. Each morning they would provide free dental work for the natives, and each evening they would share the gospel through an interpreter. At every village they visited, people trusted Christ as their Savior.

However, at the last and most remote village they came upon, there was no reaction to their message. They tried several times to help the villagers understand. After many invitations to respond, a tribal leader finally stepped forward and said, "If you are asking us to become Christians, we are not responding — because we already are!" And he proceeded to tell this story.

Several years before, one of their tribesmen murdered another man in anger. He fled into the jungle to escape the tribal punishment, which was death. He was desperately burdened under the guilt of the sin he knew he had committed. He greatly feared death either by the hands of the villagers or the harshness of the jungle, knowing that it would bring divine judgment. So he pleaded with

Divinity (whatever or whoever that was) to save him. In his jungle journey the fugitive ran into a missionary who shared with him that forgiveness can only be found through Jesus Christ. The Amazon tribesman believed the message and accepted Christ as his Savior. He returned to his village, willing to face his sentence, but with the hope of sharing his newfound faith before he was executed. As he shared his story, the other tribesmen deeply desired the forgiveness this man now knew. Soon everyone in the village accepted Christ, and the former fugitive was made the chief of a joyful community of Christians.

When Helen Keller was introduced to the story of Jesus Christ, I've heard it said that her response was "I always knew He existed, I just didn't know His name." You see, if we honestly seek Him, God has obligated Himself to send us the message of His Son.

Obviously, there is no limit to the creativity God can use to bring the message of His Son to individuals who are seeking a relationship with Him. There are many ways that a person can come to the knowledge of Jesus Christ, but there is only one way that a person can come to God — and that is through His Son, Jesus Christ.

Let me anticipate some questions I know you will eventually ask:

1. You insist that Jesus is the only way to come to God.
   Couldn't God choose to use another way?
A lot of people argue that God *could* allow people into heaven some other way, if He wanted to. "After all," they say, "He is God." They are absolutely right. But since He is God, He could choose to do it exactly the way He said He would. Right? Acts 4:12 makes it very clear that God has decided that the *only* way people can come to Him is through Jesus Christ. God does not lie.

Think about this. If people who have never heard the gospel story of Jesus Christ were able to enter God's presence in heaven some other way, then missionaries (like the apostle Paul and your grandparents) are wasting their time. Not only that, they are causing great harm by spreading the message. They are forcing innocent, ignorant humans to make a choice that could damn them to hell. Yet we are commanded all through the Bible (look at Matthew 28:19-20 and Romans 10:14-15) to spread the gospel message — that *only* through Jesus Christ can anyone have a relationship with God — "to the ends of the earth" (Acts 1:8).

2. What about children who die before they are old enough to understand God's revelation or respond to their consciences?

This is a very valid question. What does happen to babies or young children who die? Or what about people who don't have the mental capacity to understand that they need to accept Jesus as the only way to enter heaven? Well, biblical evidence points to the fact that people who are unable to consciously choose Jesus Christ during their lifetime are not held accountable in the same way we are. Second Samuel 12 tells the story of David's infant son who died just after childbirth. David was certainly destined for heaven at the end of his life. In Acts 13:22 God calls him "a man after my own heart." When David was talking about his son who had just died, he said, "I will go to him, but he will not return to me" (2 Samuel 12:23). He had no doubt that his infant child was in the presence of God.

Another example of God not holding people accountable who do not have the capacity to respond is given in Numbers 13–14. Do you remember the story of the Israelites wandering in the wilderness for forty years? This happened because they failed to trust God and did not enter the Promised Land when He intended for them to. They had sent out spies who reported back that they didn't stand a chance to make it in the new land, because the people who already occupied it were giants. So they had decided not to obey God. As a consequence God made them wander in the wilderness just outside the land for forty years — until everyone in the nation who was responsible for this sin of disobedience had died. Then the new generation obeyed God, crossed the Jordan River, and inhabited the land. In this account, all the people twenty years old and older were held responsible for the response of the nation. They had received a revelation from God, yet they chose to ignore it. However, those Israelites *under twenty years of age* were *not held accountable* for disobedience to God's revelation (see Numbers 14:29-34).

Of one fact we can be sure. God is completely fair, and in the end no one will be able to accuse Him of any unfairness. Job 34:12 says, "It is unthinkable that God would do wrong, that the Almighty would pervert justice."

3. What about the people who lived before Jesus ever came to the earth? How can they come to God through Jesus Christ since He wasn't even born yet?

The message of salvation has never changed from the time of Adam and Eve until the time we sat down to have this discussion. And it never will change! The basic truths have, and always will, remain constant:

- Man is sinful and therefore separated from holy God (see Isaiah 59:2).

- Man cannot bridge the separation by his own hard work or good deeds (see Isaiah 64:6). We'll discuss this in the next chapter.
- Therefore, man needs a redeemer (see Job 19:25).
- Man comes into a relationship with God through faith in God's promises — ultimately the promise that He would send a personal Messiah to die in man's place (see Isaiah 53:5).

The difference is that prior to Jesus coming to earth, faith was in God's future provision of a redeemer, exhibited by a present test of obedience (for example, climbing aboard an ark, trusting God to provide a promised child, sacrificing a lamb, and so on). Our faith (and everyone else's since the time of Christ) is in what He has already done through Jesus Christ.

SUMMARY

No human being can claim ignorance of the existence of God. Nor can any human being claim ignorance of personal sin. This knowledge requires a response. It is up to each individual to respond to the knowledge that he or she has received. God has obligated Himself to provide the message of salvation through Jesus Christ to those who acknowledge their need and appeal to Him for help.

The real question is not: What about those who have never heard? It is: How will those people respond to the knowledge that they have already been given?

More importantly: How will *you* respond?

QUESTION #7

ISN'T LIVING A GOOD LIFE
Good Enough?

DO YOU REMEMBER THE SUNNY SUMMER DAY MANY YEARS AGO WHEN ALL four of you got together with some other boys in the neighborhood and decided to form a club? It was a very exclusive club, open to only the most elite athletes in the neighborhood. I don't remember the exact name you gave it, but it was something like "Only for Awesome Athletes" or "Just for Jocks." After intense discussion and animated debate it was decided that the criterion for membership would be the timed running of an obstacle course that you would design together.

You spent all morning planning the course. The picnic table was turned on its side to present a wall; benches were lined up to form a meandering tightrope course; ropes were hung from tree branches; swings were lifted to their highest notches; and a tunnel was created from old boxes and barrels. A stopwatch was found and a much argued cutoff time was announced. (I think it was ninety seconds.) A few practice runs were made, and initiation activities began.

Zach, being the chief architect and one of the oldest at age ten, was the first to go. He made the course look easy. Matthew, more than likely the instigator of the whole venture, followed. Some of the bigger neighborhood boys who had joined in did just fine. Then it was Ben's turn. He was only six. It took him several tries, but he finally completed the course within the time limit. Jonathan, who was only three years old at the time, didn't even come close. He tried and tried, but there was no way he could hurdle all the obstacles, weave his way through the mazes, and swing across the ditches in less than ninety seconds. He was devastated. So were several girls who showed up, vied for admission, and failed.

After everyone had been given adequate opportunity to qualify, seven guys went running off into the woods to build a clubhouse and enjoy the benefits of their elite stature — leaving one little boy named Jonathan and a few young ladies standing in the middle of our backyard in tears.

Standards must be met for admission into just about every organization in our society. Almost everyone understands this and accepts it (except sometimes when they're the ones left standing outside). And anyone I have ever talked to agrees that there most definitely must be a standard for admission into heaven. Otherwise it could not possibly remain the sin-free paradise we all want to live in and enjoy one day. Which leads to the all-important question . . .

THE QUESTION: WHAT IS THE STANDARD TO GET INTO HEAVEN?

If you ask most people what they think the standard is for acceptance into heaven, they reply something like, "Well, you have to live a good life." When you try to narrow them down by asking, "How good?" they usually hesitate and blurt out something rather random like, "Well, better than average," or "You just really have to do your best." So you try to get more specific. "How often do you have to do your best?" you ask. "Well, most of the time," is the usual response.

The standards most people set for admission into heaven are very hazy, extremely arbitrary, and almost always inconsistent. They are hardly ever clear and simple like the measurement you used for entrance into your backyard club. There are so many questions left unanswered.

If a person can get to heaven by living a good life, how good does that person need to be? And by what set of rules will that goodness be judged? Are we talking about the Golden Rule or the Ten Commandments or the Five Pillars of Islam? And how often does that person need to do his or her very best? Would 50.1 percent of the time be enough? That covers being good MOST of the time. Or should we make it 75 percent of the time in order to keep heaven a little more pure? And which good works count for how much? Does helping a little old lady across the street count as much as sending money to starving kids in war-torn countries? How about being kind to your little brother? Or is that something that is just expected and therefore not worth very much?

This is all very confusing. The more specific we try to get in developing a works system to get us into heaven, the more difficult it becomes to develop what everyone would consider to be a fair, unbiased rating scale. Any criteria we come up with seems to be subject to how each individual personally views the situation. The only consistent factor I can find in manmade criteria for acceptance into heaven is that each person places the cutoff point for entrance into his exclusive "Heaven Club" a little below the level he thinks he can attain.

But the question really isn't, "How good do you or I think we should be to get into heaven?" It is, "How good does God think we should be?" After all, heaven is His home.

Suppose each of us could build a tower with our good works, the height of each tower being proportionate to the good deeds we perform while here on earth. Let's say our target is the moon. We'll pretend that that's where God is, and if we can construct a tower high enough to reach the moon, then we can get into heaven.

As we build our own towers we start to look around to see how others are doing. We see the tower of the big kid next door. He started off real well. There were lots of good works that went into his construction at first — when he was a Boy Scout, and on safety patrol at school, and a member of a service club in high school. But lately, now that he's in college, it seems that his building progress has gone into slow motion.

Across town we see a very tall tower, a real skyscraper, and we presume it belongs to the pastor of our church or the head of the Boys' Club in town.

We notice some construction sites where the workers appear to spend more time digging than actually building. They have hollowed out craters for their foundations and never even reached ground level. The deepest holes belong to people like Jack the Ripper and Adolf Hitler. Basically, we notice that huge differences exist in the heights of the various towers surrounding us based on the large discrepancies in the amount of good works performed.

Now suppose God lived on the moon and we could join Him as He inspects our building progress from His vantage point. We would no doubt discover that all the towers appear very similar to Him as He views them from above. The differences would be miniscule at best.

Although there are huge distinctions between the heights of the towers, an enormous chasm of space separates even the tallest manmade building from its destination. It is extremely discouraging to realize that even the highest tower on the horizon — possibly the one built by Mother Teresa — is nowhere close to reaching the moon. (And she has already passed away, leaving no more opportunities to build!)

The point I am making is this: There are great differences in human levels of goodness and achievement, but all of them fall short of reaching God's cutoff point. "What is that cutoff point?" you ask. Ah, therein lies the problem. You see, God's standard — His cutoff point for allowing us into heaven — is *perfection*.

THE PROBLEM: GOD'S STANDARD IS PERFECTION AND WE ARE NOT PERFECT

Jesus makes it very clear in Matthew 5:48 that we must be *perfect* if we want to enter into heaven. The scribes and Pharisees who spent their whole lives striving to live up to extreme standards of goodness weren't even close to good enough! Jesus said that unless our righteousness exceeds theirs we don't stand a chance of getting in (see Matthew 5:20). God used the word *blameless* when He described His requirements to Abraham (see Genesis 17:1). And to Moses He commanded, "Be holy because I, the LORD your God, am holy" (Leviticus 19:2). Peter reiterates the need for holiness in the New Testament (see 1 Peter 1:16), and, as I already mentioned, Jesus, in Matthew 5:48 tells us we must be perfect, just as God is perfect, if we want to enter heaven with Him.

Heaven is not a place of minimal sin. Heaven is a place where there is *no* sin. If even the tiniest smidgen of sin was introduced, heaven's purity would be contaminated, and God would be forced to compromise His holiness. Isaiah 59:2 tells us that anything less than perfect must be separated from God in order to keep His holiness intact. Even if He allowed the very best of the best of us in, based on our good works, God would be allowing imperfection to infiltrate His perfection. Not one of us can do good things or behave perfectly 100 percent of the time no matter how hard we try. Romans 3:23 states it very plainly: All of us have sinned and fallen far short of God's perfect standard.

I'd go so far as to say that I don't know a single person who could make it through twenty-four hours of perfect living. Do you? If some kind of camcorder could videotape us *and our thoughts*, we'd probably be forced to admit we couldn't last for even two hours. If we were allowed to enter heaven, every one of us would corrupt it in just the same way one drop of arsenic corrupts a whole glass of pure water. Ninety-nine point nine percent perfect is not perfect at all!

Do you remember the story of Noah? God wiped out almost all of the evil in the world, saving only a few animals and eight human beings. The world should have been a pretty wonderful place to live once the land dried up. Yet within a very short time (about the length of time it took Noah to grow a few grapes and turn them into wine), sin infiltrated the world and soon it was just as disgusting a place as it had been before.

No, living a good life is not enough to get us into heaven. Even living a *very, very* good life won't do the trick. You see, it really isn't a lack of goodness on our part that separates us from God. It's the presence of *any* evil (sin) at all! So, how can we possibly hope to go to heaven when we die? Ahhh, God has provided a solution!

THE SOLUTION: GOD SENT A PERFECT SUBSTITUTE TO PAY THE PENALTY FOR OUR SIN

If you have never read 2 Corinthians 5:21, you need to open your Bible to it right now and underline it. I'll quote it for you, but I want you to claim it as your very own verse. It is one of the most exciting sentences in the Bible.

God made him (Jesus) who had no sin to be sin for us, so that in him we might become the righteousness of God.

Wow! Christ lived a perfect, sinless life (the life we admit that none of us could live) while He was here on earth. When He died on the cross, He died as the perfect sacrifice in our place, accepting the penalty for our sin, which is separation from God and the inability to enter His presence. For several horrible, gruesome hours Jesus endured the torture of having His father, God, turn His back on Him. When we accept Christ's substitution for us, God no longer sees the sin in our lives. It has been exchanged for Christ's perfect righteousness. All He sees is His Son's holiness! We are declared perfect! Sinless! Acceptable in God's presence! Free to enter heaven!

I am told that a story appeared in the *Los Angeles Times* several years ago concerning a judge named Goldstein and his son. Judge Goldstein was known for his very harsh demands for justice. He always handed out the longest sentence or the highest fine allowed by the law, earning him the reputation as "The Hanging Judge." One day a reporter for the *Los Angeles Times* was reading through the court dockets and happened to notice that a young man arrested for drunk driving was going to appear in The Hanging Judge's courtroom the next day. The young man also had the last name of Goldstein. A little investigation led the reporter to the discovery that this young man was indeed Judge Goldstein's own son.

The headline in the newspaper the next morning blared: *Will the Hanging Judge Hang His Own Son?* The courtroom was packed as young Goldstein approached the bench. The judge read the charges, accepted the guilty plea, and, sure enough, he handed out the strictest penalty allowed by law. "As the judge in this case I impose the harshest penalty the law allows. You will need to present the bailiff with a check for $200, otherwise you will go to jail!" he bellowed, slamming down the gavel to signify that the case was complete.

Then Judge Goldstein stood up, stepped out from behind the bench, took off his robe, and walked around to where his son stood with his head down before the bailiff. The judge placed his arm around the teenager's shoulders. "As your father, who loves you, I have a check already made out to the court in the sum of $200. Your penalty has been paid in full," he said softly, hugging his son to signify that his love was unconditional.

This story illustrates exactly what God has done for us. He demands holiness. We fail. We must be judged. But He has already paid the penalty for us by sending His Son Jesus to die in our place. Justice is satisfied while God's love is demonstrated.

No, none of the righteous things that we ever do will save us from the penalty of sin and allow us to go to heaven. It is only by God's mercy that we will ever call heaven our home (see Titus 3:5)!

There is a really neat ending to the story I started to tell you about the backyard club that was formed on that hot summer day several years ago. Soon after the seven big guys went running off into the woods to build a clubhouse and enjoy the benefits of their elite stature as world-renowned (well, at least neighborhood-renowned) athletes, they all came running back. They found little Jonathan, totally dismayed and dejected, sitting under a tiny oak tree. Zach ran up to him, knelt down, and told Jonathan to jump on his back. And while Matthew timed them, Zach ran the obstacle course. With all the guys cheering, Zach made it with Jonathan on his back from start to finish in the required amount of time.

Jonathan was in! He had all the rights and privileges of any member of the awesomest athletes' club in Polk County, Florida! What he couldn't possibly have earned on his own, he was allowed to enjoy based on what his brother had done for him. All he had to do was believe Zach could do it for him and crawl onto his brother's back.

All religions other than Christianity are essentially do-it-yourself propositions. They provide a list of rules. "Follow these," they say, "and you will find favor with God, and eventually you will have access to heaven." Paul E. Little, in *Know Why You Believe*, said that in reality all other religious systems are no more than sets of swimming instructions for drowning men. Christianity, however, is a life-preserver.[1]

If we all lined up on the coast of California and had to swim to Hawaii, none of us would make it. Oh, some of you would get a whole lot farther off shore than I would, but not a single person could possibly make it to the Hawaiian shore on his own. We all would need someone to come along in a boat and rescue us or we would drown.

When Christ died on the cross in our place, He essentially came along in a boat and offered to take us where we couldn't get on our own. He rescued us. He is our only means of salvation (as we said in answering Question #5). If we will just believe Him and get on board, He will take us to heaven.

That brings up another question: What does it really mean to *believe*? We won't go into that right now, but I promise you we will look at this closely in a few more chapters (Question #10). Meanwhile, here are a couple of other questions that will possibly come up as you think over what we have talked about in this chapter.

1. Since good works don't get us into heaven and the penalty
   for our bad works is already paid for, we could just live rotten lives and not worry about it. Right?

Second Corinthians 5:17 tells us that when we accept Christ, and
what He did on the cross for us, things change inside: "Therefore,
if anyone is in Christ, he is a *new* creation; the old has gone, the
new has come!" (emphasis mine). It's as if we had been criminals,
but were granted parole instead of having to go to death row. But
the parole officer in charge of monitoring our behavior comes to
live inside of us (instead of in some office near city hall) so that
he can constantly be there to help us make wise decisions. The
parole officer is called the Holy Spirit. He helps us fight any desires
to do wrong and convinces us to live righteously (see Galatians
5:16-17). If we accept God's solution for our sin problem, we will
want to live good lives in thankfulness for what Christ did for us
on the cross. Ephesians 2:8-10 says:

> For it is by grace you have been saved, through faith —
> and this not from yourselves, it is the gift of God — not
> by works, so that no one can boast. For we are God's
> workmanship, created in Christ Jesus to do good
> works, which God prepared in advance for us to do.

You see, good works aren't what get us into heaven. But they
are what God has designed for us to do once we accept His gift of
eternal life in heaven.

2. What about reincarnation? How does that fit with
   Christianity?

Very simply put, the goal of reincarnation is the continuous recy-
cling of one's soul from body to body, each time trying to live a

purer life (building better karma), until one day the soul attains a state of perfection and sinlessness and enters into a glorious nothingness called nirvana. (Why anyone would work so hard to be obliterated is beyond me!) Sin is paid for in this system by suffering along the way. Effort and good works, however, lead to purification and advancement to a higher, more perfect soul experience. In other words, if a cat is really bad it might come back as a roach, or if the water boy is a really good servant, he might come back as the star football player.

Most reincarnationists believe that all the souls that will ever be created are already in existence. They merely migrate from one external form to another. This fact raises several questions in my mind:

- Why does there seem to be more and more evil in the world rather than less if these souls are all striving for perfection?
- Why does the population on our planet increase rather than decrease if souls are constantly reaching the perfect state of nirvana? And shouldn't some of the lower life forms be disappearing or decreasing?
- How on earth does a grub worm or a roach build better karma?

The whole idea of reincarnation contradicts the Bible. Hebrews 9:27 tells us that man is destined to die *once* and after that he is judged as to whether or not he should be allowed into heaven. (Verse 28 tells us once again that it is only Jesus' sacrifice on the cross that can take away our sin and allow us to enter God's presence.)

One more interesting note about reincarnation. The fact that several "celebrities" in our culture adhere to this religious belief and claim to have concrete, "inside" knowledge of past lives that they have lived should not surprise us. If we truly believe that the Bible is God's Word (as we discussed in answering Question #3), we must also believe that there are demonic forces at work in our world. It would not be at all impossible for an evil spirit who inhabited a life several centuries ago to reinhabit another life today, bringing with it firsthand knowledge of past circumstances and events. To use this as evidence for the existence of reincarnation, however, is totally erroneous.

SUMMARY

Any standard we try to apply to determine a cutoff point that should allow us access into heaven turns out to be arbitrary and opinionated. Any efforts we make to live up to our standards are based on pride in our own abilities. Instead of acknowledging that we cannot live a good enough life on our own, we devise all kinds of methods and rituals to get us there. This was Gandhi's problem (as well as Buddha's and Mohammed's and Krishna's and Joseph Smith's and mine for many years). Gandhi, the zealously practicing Hindu I mentioned in Question #6, thought that somehow he could become pure enough to be accepted by God based on his own good works and hard effort. This is what he said at the very end of his life:

> But the path of self-purification is hard and steep. To attain to perfect purity one has to become absolutely passion-free in thought, speech and action; to rise above the opposing currents of love and hatred, attachment and repulsion. I know that I have not in me as yet that triple purity, in spite of constant ceaseless striving for it. That is why the world's praise fails to move me, indeed it very often stings me. To conquer the subtle

passions seems to me to be harder far than the physical conquest of the world by the force of arms.[2]

What a sad conclusion to the life of a man who dedicated his whole adulthood to attaining purity!

Trying to build a ladder to get ourselves into heaven based on our good works is more futile than trying to build a ladder to the moon out of Lego blocks.

A system of works always brings frustration and failure, whereas Christ offers forgiveness and freedom. The choice is ours.[3]

God's standard is perfection. We all sin and fall very short of this standard and are, therefore, incapable of gaining entrance into His presence. Our sin separates us from God. But God has provided a solution through the perfect, sinless life and death of His Son Jesus. Jesus' death and separation from God on the cross in our place pays our penalty and satisfies God's justice. It also demonstrates God's unbelievable love!

QUESTION #8

ISN'T CHISTIANITY JUST A
Psychological Crutch?

THIS SEEMS TO BE A VERY STRAIGHTFORWARD QUESTION. THE PERSON doing the asking obviously expects an uncomplicated yes or no answer, right? And judging by the smirk on his or her face, you can usually tell which answer is expected! But as simple as it is to ask, it is a question I could not answer for most of my teenage years. I wrestled hard and long with its implications and finally came to a conclusion. It took me many more years to realize that the answer I had arrived at was 180 degrees wrong!

You see, my first semester in college I was introduced to a book called *The Psychology of Religious Experience*. (I mentioned this in the Introduction.) As I read it, I thought I had found the answer to every burning question I had ever had about Christianity in one simple summary statement: All religions are merely psychological crutches.

After reading it several times, I came to the conclusion that the author (Erwin P. Goodenough) was correct. He taught that all religions were merely coping mechanisms that had been intricately developed over the centuries. He believed that this was particularly true of religions based on the Christian principles and practices — like the one I had been raised to believe. According to his theory, my parents, and many others like them, chose to follow certain messages and mandates of the Bible because by believing and obeying them they found psychological resolve and strength to help them deal with their inadequacies and overcome their own weaknesses and pain. If I chose to accept the same belief system they had (only because I had been preconditioned by my upbringing to do so) I, too, would be admitting my own insufficiencies.

This all seemed to make sense to me and I began to agree with the author that all religions could function equally effectively. Their success or failure was basically dependent on the culture in which they took root. I smugly contended that if I wanted to, I could start a religion based on the healing powers of praying to a potted petunia. All I had to do was convince people to believe in my plant, to trust that any prayers made while kneeling before it could change their lives. I'm sure that, based on their belief, the "potted plant pray-ers" would soon begin to rationalize and attribute any changes that took place in their lives to their newfound faith in potted petunias. They would no doubt spread the word and soon people all over the world would be buying petunias and praying to potted plants. I figured that if I took my practice to Africa, I could stimulate just as much change in people's lives as my parents had when they introduced Christianity.

I began to define all religions, including the biblical Christianity my parents had embraced, as crutches. They were merely means of support for people who were in some way handicapped by fear or their own inadequacies. I felt that any help that they derived from these crutches was purely psychological. In other words, I thought all religion was subjective — "a thing of the mind" — with no objective data or results to back it up.

However, just because I had discovered that they were really shams didn't mean that I thought we should do away with all religions. I realized that crutches can come in handy sometimes, and I felt that religion could be every bit as useful to a mind with a need as a wooden crutch is to a body with a need. However, *I* didn't need religion. "A healthy mind like mine has no need for a crutch," I proudly asserted. "I am much too strong to need such assistance!"

It was only when I honestly began to investigate the questions that we have already studied in this book, and truly took the time to examine the claims of Christianity, that I realized how foolish I had been. I began to understand that there were two major problems with my theory:

1. I was clueless when it came to understanding my own weaknesses and need for outside assistance.
2. I didn't understand the objective evidences and concrete data that support Christianity.

I now know the true answer to the question, "Isn't Christianity just a psychological crutch?" And I'm excited that I have an opportunity to share it with you!

THE ANSWER IS "YES AND NO"!

Whoa! You didn't expect that, did you? Actually my answer isn't a cop-out. It truly is the right response. Part of the problem we run across in trying to respond to this question is that it cannot be satisfied by a simple yes or no answer. You see, in a sense Christianity *is* a crutch, one we all need because we are all weak. So *yes*, Christianity is a crutch. However, it is not *just* a crutch, nor is it *psychological.* It is not merely a personal, subjective belief — one that exists only in the individual's mind. It is backed by valid, objective, universal evidence.

Let's study this together. We'll look at the psychological part first.

CHRISTIANITY *IS NOT* "PSYCHOLOGICAL"

While discussing the answer to Question #1, we talked about the physical evidences for the existence of God. Among other things we looked at the reality of motion and pointed to the intricate design of the universe. Both point to the necessity and reality of a Supreme Being.

In answering Question #3 we discussed some of the historical and archaeological evidences that verify the accounts recorded in the Bible. We also examined proofs for the validity of the manuscripts in which they are recorded.

In answering Question #4 we discovered the reliability of the miracles and the soundness of the Resurrection accounts. The resurrection of Jesus Christ is the core of all of Christianity. It is the jugular vein. If the Resurrection is true, then so is Christianity. The evidences presented in that chapter establish the occurrence of the Resurrection beyond a reasonable doubt. Our faith is based on objective realities — not subjective thoughts or feelings.

These are just a few of the factors that confirm that the biblical basis for Christianity is concretely reliable. It is unfair for anyone to judge it as merely a personal bias based on emotional experiences and preconditioning. For me to dismiss Christianity as invalid just because I was predisposed to believe it by my upbringing is simply not justifiable. There are many things I was preconditioned to believe as a young child that I later negated as I matured and discovered the truth. Take for instance Santa Claus and the Tooth Fairy. And I don't ever recall running outside on Easter mornings to search for the Easter Bunny once I was a teenager. On the flip side, many things that I was conditioned to believe always were and always will be true. The fact that the stovetop can get hot enough to burn my hand or that sharp knives can cut my fingers are still valid facts in my life today. Just because I was brought up believing something does not make it right or wrong.

No, preconditioning and emotional experience have nothing at all to do with the validity or invalidity of a belief. Christianity is based on facts and findings. I would challenge you to go back and reread Questions #1 through #4 if you still find this hard to accept. Christianity is definitely not just "a thing of the mind."

Not only is Christianity substantiated by physical, historical, and archaeological evidences, there are social evidences as well. Dr. Guenter Lewy, currently a professor at the University of Massachusetts, is not a believer in Christian principles and practice. As a matter of fact, when he began to write his most recent book, he planned to title it something like *Why America Doesn't Need Religion*. He wanted it to be "a defense of secular humanism and ethical relativism."[1] In other words, he wanted to prove that human beings (rather than some god they contrived) are the best authorities to decide what society could and should do. Furthermore, the decisions that humans make should be based on the circumstances at the time rather than on some outdated code of conduct (like the Bible) that was developed at a less sophisticated, more superstitious time in history. He felt that society would be much better off to do away with the concept of God completely.

However, as Lewy began to study Christianity, his research caused him to reverse his position 180 degrees. He found that Christianity has historically been a major impetus for the support of human dignity and social justice. He found that rates of marital conflict, divorce, births to unwed mothers, juvenile delinquency, adult crime, racial prejudice, and other "indicators of moral failure and social ills" decreased among believing Christians.[2] Dr. Lewy actually concluded at the end of his study that Christianity is vital to creating a healthy, humane society and that living by biblical principles makes people healthier and happier. The book he ended up writing is titled *Why America Needs Religion*. Wow! What a startling reversal!

Many social movements began when individuals demanded that society live by the principles found in the Bible. William Wilberforce, the man most responsible for the abolition of slavery in England, and Abraham Lincoln, whose courage put an end to slavery in the United States, both found their strength in Christian teachings. Civil rights movements in many nations have been initiated by people of faith.

When anyone investigates it thoroughly, objective data and results always validate Christianity. The minds that reject it are the minds that have not explored it honestly and fairly.

CHRISTIANITY *IS* A CRUTCH

As anyone who has ever met him knows, Jonathan has always tried to keep up with his big brothers. Although he is several years younger than the rest of you, he has attempted to reach your standards in everything from sleeping in a big boy bed, to riding a bicycle, to reading at a young age, to playing baseball.

When Jonathan was eleven years old, he played Little League baseball. Zach and Matthew played for the high school baseball team, and Ben was on the junior high team. Every day that he was not scheduled to attend his own practice, Jonathan would practice with one of your "big boy" teams. He was not about to be left behind or treated like a lesser ball player.

One day he was out shagging balls while you older boys took batting practice. Tired of running from one side of the out-field to the other, he asked the high school coach if he could borrow the golf cart to retrieve the balls. The coach laughed at his ingenuity and said something like, "Sure, why not! There's nothing out there you can run into except the fence."

It was an omen! Sure enough — as Jonathan rode close enough to the outfield fence to scoop up a hard-hit ball, his dangling foot got caught in the chain link. He tried desperately to kick it loose as the golf cart kept moving, but only succeeded in lodging it even further in the meshing. As the cart continued moving, his leg was twisted, and he was left lying in a huddled, hurting heap. It was quite evident that the spiraling action had snapped both of the bones below his knee.

For several days Jonathan was confined to a wheelchair with a cast from his hip to his toes. Then as the pain lessened and his leg began to heal, he was given a pair of crutches. In a matter of days Jonathan became very agile on those crutches. He got so good that soon he could do 360s without putting either leg down. One day his teacher called me and begged me to encourage him to use his good leg for balance as he maneuvered down the hallway. It made her nervous to see him walk the whole length of the hallway using only his crutches — without the balance or stabilization of either leg hitting the floor. (She was also concerned that he might be showing off a little!)

Those two pieces of wood that had previously hung on the wall of the supply closet at the medical clinic took on great value in Jonathan's life. They became his transportation, his strength, his connection to others. They became very useful — even indispensable. They made his life more fun.

Then one day the doctor declared that Jonathan's bones had

healed very well and he would have no further use for crutches. Although they had been a necessity during the mending process, once the break was completely healed and the pain and weakness had vanished, they were no longer necessary.

To use a crutch is to admit that a problem exists and then to accept assistance. That's what Jonathan did. If we were completely whole in this broken world, we wouldn't need help. However, not one of us can claim to be completely whole spiritually (remember Question #7?). We all have handicaps such as impatience, anger, fear, irritability, pride, dishonesty, and on and on. Not a single one of us could walk up to the pearly gates of heaven on our own, stand before a holy God, and explain why He should allow our sinful little self into His awesomely pure presence. We all need help. Every one of us must rely on Jesus and what He has done for us.

In the same way that Jonathan needed his crutches to lean on due to his pain and the weakness of his bones, we need our faith to lean on. But one day we will enter God's presence and be made completely whole. We will no longer have any weaknesses or imperfections. We will no longer need a crutch to lean on. But until then, we should allow our faith in God and His Word to provide us with all the strength that it can.

For centuries major skeptics of religion such as Jean-Paul Sartre, Bertrand Russell, Karl Marx, Sigmund Freud, and Jesse Ventura (I'm kidding about his stature, but not about his beliefs) have portrayed religion as nothing more than a help for the emotionally weak who fear the future. (Ventura, as governor of Minnesota, became the spokesman for skepticism when he publicly stated in November of 1999 that Christianity is just "a sham and a crutch for weak-minded people.") All of these men failed to acknowledge their need for help. Their intellectual pride got in the way of their investigations and did not allow them to see their own faults. They failed to look at the facts, and mostly they failed to look at their own miserable lives. If they had, they would have seen that they, too, were leaning on crutches — crutches that were not nearly as stable and objective as Christianity. They were relying on their own intellect and reason.

For several years after I graduated from college, I leaned on my own hard work and the efforts I put into my job as a school nurse and health educator in the west Dallas housing projects to bring me fulfillment and satisfaction. It was truly a labor of love. It was always difficult and sometimes dangerous. But I took great pride in all that I accomplished in the lives of the family-torn children I served.

I got up early each morning to avoid the snarling traffic of the Dallas highway system. I spent the hour before the students arrived researching and studying social issues and diseases. I spent the next eight hours caring for unhealthy children, diagnosing illnesses, and dispensing medication. I spent my own money developing programs and projects that would interest and influence the children to better health habits and care. I trudged through rat-infested alleys to find children I knew needed help and to argue with parents who did not understand their needs. I went home exhausted each evening only to return again the following morning and start all over.

I felt like the Mother Teresa of George Washington Carver Elementary School. If I wasn't doing enough good things to get myself into heaven, nobody was!

Then one morning I didn't want to get up. I was too exhausted. I was tired of argumentative parents and disgusted with snotty-nosed children. I didn't want to learn one more thing about communicable diseases or design one more health-care project. I just wanted to stay in my own clean, white sheets and sleep the day away. I realized that day that I wasn't nearly the angel of mercy I had begun to think I was.

I had been leaning on a crutch — my own good works — and that morning it broke! It snapped right in two, leaving me lying flat on the ground. (Actually, it left me lying in my bed for several hours!) My own good deeds didn't give me nearly the fulfillment or satisfaction or peace that I thought they always would. They couldn't hold me up anymore.

You see, the question isn't, "Should we or should we not use crutches to get us through life?" We all use them. Everyone (including Sartre, Russell, Marx, Freud, and Jesse Ventura!) leans on something to bring him happiness and fulfillment in life. The question is, "What crutch should we use? What crutch is strong enough to really support us? What crutch won't break when we lean on it with all our weight?" Belief is only as valid as the object it is placed in.

You may have heard the story told about the two men who went hunting in Colorado one January day. Let's call them Billy and Bubba. Dusk fell suddenly and their only chance to get back to the hunting lodge before dark was to cut across a big lake. So Billy stepped onto the ice and started to walk across. But Bubba was from the South. He had never been to Colorado in the winter before. He was afraid the ice would not support him and he stood motionless at the side of the lake. Billy, who had been there many times before during the cold winter months, turned around and informed Bubba that the ice was at least three feet thick and it could easily support his weight. Then he continued to stride across the lake.

Bubba was scared to death. Slowly he began to inch his way across, first on his hands and knees, then shuffling on his feet. As his confidence grew he became more surefooted, and he and Billy both arrived at the lodge well before sundown.

The two men went back to hunt in Colorado later that spring. Once again the sun began to set. Once again they were on the opposite side of the lake from the lodge. But this time it was Bubba who, seeing ice covering the lake, started walking across.

"No! No!" Billy hollered to his confident friend. "It's late May and the ice is probably no thicker than a quarter of an inch!"

Bubba, however, paid no attention. Continuing with great faith in the ability of the ice to hold him up, he ventured on. A few feet from shore the ice cracked, and Bubba fell spluttering and splattering into the chilly water.

Bubba's faith was much stronger the second time he approached the lake than it had been the first. However the *object* of his faith was far less sound. No matter how much he believed in its strength, that quarter-inch thickness of ice could not hold him up.

Our faith is only as good as the object we place it in. As we have learned, the basis for Christianity is strong and objective. It will hold us up through all that life has to offer. A potted plant, a religion based on our own good works, reliance on another human being or our own intellect — these things can only let us down. One day they will crack, and we will crash. We will be left floundering, the startled victims of an inadequate object of faith.

BUT CHRISTIANITY IS MORE, MUCH MORE THAN *JUST* A CRUTCH

Earlier we said that by using a crutch we acknowledge our own inadequacies and weaknesses. But Christ doesn't offer us only a crutch. He offers us a **CURE!** The penalty for our sins (our inadequacies and weaknesses) is death — separation from a perfect, holy God for all of eternity. Christ substituted His life as payment for our sin so that we can enter God's presence (we talked about this in Question #7). As long as we live on this earth, we will continue to stumble and sin. But one day, when we enter His holy presence in heaven, we will become pure and whole. We will be healed! (Let's talk more about heaven in the next chapter.)

When my parents were missionaries in Africa, my father frequently was called on to provide medical care. Though he had only minimal training, he knew more about disease and death than most of the people he worked with. So he was always the one called into duty when health was on the line. One of the native medical practices bothered him very much. Whenever someone had a large swelling or infection, the medicine men would incise the area around it, place a suction device over the incision (usually the horn of a cow or goat), and drain as much blood as possible. Called bloodletting, this common practice seemed to greatly reduce the swelling and relieve the pain.

My father, however, tried to convince the medicine men that what their patients really needed in most cases was antibiotics, not loss of blood. He insisted that the infections would return if not treated properly, but no one seemed to listen to him. The few times he convinced patients to take antibiotics, they returned to the medicine man the next day complaining that their symptoms had not been relieved by my father's "magic" pills.

Because the bloodletting provided immediate relief, the patients presumed that healing had taken place. It didn't matter to them that the relief was temporary. They just kept trying it over and over — very often until they died. Relief with the use of antibiotics took several days. However, my father was finally able to convince a few of the Africans of their long-term effectiveness, and soon he was inundated with patients.

One method of healing (bloodletting) provided immediate,

albeit short-term comfort. The other (the use of antibiotics) provided a cure. I might *feel* better if I believed in Mohammed or Buddha or my own good works or my potted plant. But they are all like bloodletting. The feeling of wellness is only temporary. I could actually be getting worse while I think I'm getting better. Jesus Christ provides a cure — a permanent guarantee of wellness and wholeness! And, as we have already learned, we base our trust in Him on a firm foundation of objective facts and findings.

SUMMARY

Christianity is not a belief system based on emotions or preconditioning. It is not psychological. Christianity, when honestly investigated and evaluated, is firmly grounded by historical and scientific facts and findings.

All of us are spiritually sick and in need of help. We cannot make it into God's holy presence in heaven on our own. If we want to call Christianity (the belief that Jesus died in our place and rose again and paid the penalty for our sins) a crutch, that is okay. But we must realize that it is more, much more, than *just* a crutch. Christianity offers a cure, a promise of wholeness and perfection when we enter God's heavenly presence.

QUESTION #9

IS THERE REALLY A HELL?
What About Heaven?

WE WERE WATCHING A GAME SHOW THE OTHER NIGHT. THE MAN IN THE hot seat had already won $125,000. On the line was another $125,000. If the man answered a multiple-choice question correctly, he would be pretty well set for the next several years of his life. Plus he would have a chance to go for $500,000 and a possible million dollars. Wow! However, if he answered incorrectly he would lose most of what he had already earned, and he would leave the studio with little more than the cash to cover his airfare and expenses. Talk about pressure!

But there was another option — sort of an escape route. The man could choose to walk away. If he did not attempt to answer the question at all, he could just pocket the $125,000 he had already won. He expressed that he had a lot of debt and could really use the $125,000 to pay off his new house. "But on the other hand," he agonized, "a lot more money would mean a lot more fun."

There were huge monetary consequences to the choice the man was about to make. He was definitely sweating under the hot lights in the studio!

We saw in the answer to Question #2 that life is filled with such dilemmas. There are consequences to every choice we make in life. Some are much more severe than others. The magnitude of the choice is determined by its consequences. (Remember the story about choosing a glass of Coke or a glass of Pepsi versus drinking a glass of Coke or a glass of Clorox?)

The book of Genesis tells us that when God created Adam and Eve they were perfect — flawless. Not a single thing was wrong with them physically, mentally, emotionally, or spiritually. And the world God placed them in was completely free from any evil or suffering. As a matter of fact, Genesis 1:31 tells us that when God saw all that He had created, He declared out loud to the whole universe that it was VERY good!

Although God loved them very much and wanted more than anything else to enjoy loving fellowship with them, He did not want to *force* His love on His created beings. So He made Adam and Eve with the ability to make choices. They could freely choose to love or reject their Creator. If He had offered no options, God's creatures would have been nothing more than robots going through the motions of love. All of their reactions would have been pre-programmed. All of their responses would have been prescribed. You see, the capacity to make choices is essential to any relationship. So God gave Adam and Eve the privilege of choosing whether or not they would love and obey Him.

That choice, of course, had consequences. If Adam and Eve chose to love and accept a relationship with God and all the gifts He so lavishly wanted to give them, they would have fellowship with Him and blessings beyond anything they could ever imagine.

But if they chose to reject God and His commandments, they would have to be separated from His presence. That would mean not only an end to their physical life on this planet, but spiritual death as well, because they would be severed from the source of all spiritual life — God Himself. They would sentence themselves to a life apart from Him.

It was a humongous decision, one of great magnitude and significance!

Unfortunately, Adam and Eve chose to disregard God. They disobeyed His commands and ate the fruit He had forbidden. Imperfection entered the planet for the first time and with it the pain and suffering we now know. The temporal consequences (those we experience here on earth) are bad enough, but the eternal consequences are devastating. The entire human race descended from Adam and Eve, and therefore every one of us was born into a state of separation from God. (You can look back at Question #2 for more about how this came to be.)

But the story doesn't end there. As we have mentioned several times already, God offers us another option. There is a way to escape the horrible consequences of Adam and Eve's decision. God sent His own Son, Jesus, to take our place. He lived a perfect life here on earth, then died a sacrificial death in our place. He suffered not only physical death, but also spiritual separation from God. If we accept His payment for us, we will be declared clean and pure and flawless and worthy of entering God's holy presence.

Pretend two plates are on a table in front of you. On one of them — let's say the one on the left — is an Oreo cookie. The plate represents you, and the Oreo is the sin in your life. On the other plate — obviously the one on the right — is a vanilla wafer. They represent Jesus and His holiness. Now, in your mind, switch the Oreo cookie and the vanilla wafer. The plates remain right where they are. When God looks down at you (the plate on the left), what does He see? He sees the vanilla wafer. You see, Christ not only wants to take your sin away (the Oreo cookie), He wants to replace it with His righteousness (the vanilla wafer). If you receive Christ's payment for your sins, when God looks at you He no longer sees your sin. He sees Christ's holiness in its place, and He announces for everyone in heaven to hear, "Jonathan (or Ben, or Matthew, or Zach, or whoever you are) is perfect. Let him come on in and enjoy My presence!"

Unfortunately not everyone accepts God's way out. They sadly and mistakenly think they are doing pretty well on their own. They want to keep trying to get more out of life themselves, when actually they are doomed to failure.

Just as a wonderful life in heaven forever with the King of the universe is the consequence of accepting God's escape route, there is a consequence for rejection. That brings us to a subject we hate to discuss — a place of eternal separation from God, a place we call hell. Is there really such a place? Could God actually sentence anyone to an eternity of torment? Let's try to justify hell from God's point of view.

THE LOVING JUSTICE OF HELL

God could have decided to do several things with those who choose to reject Him and disobey His commandments.

First of all, God could have chosen to ignore their wrongdoings. After all, how could a loving God sentence His created beings to an eternity of suffering?

Well, let me tell you a story. Back when Jonathan was about three years old, he could be quite a little pain. One of Ben and Matthew's favorite pastimes was to stack up blocks and create monstrously tall towers. One of Jonathan's favorite pastimes, on the other hand, was to knock them down. As soon as you guys would complete one section of your creation, Jonathan would sneak into the room and kick the tower, scattering blocks clear across the room.

We pleaded with Jonathan not to destroy the structures. That didn't work. We gave him his own separate activity to enjoy — to no avail. We tried to include him in the block-building endeavor. Once again our efforts were useless. Jonathan continued to take great pleasure in the destruction rather than the construction of block buildings.

We finally gave Jonathan an alternative. If he chose not to touch the tower he could stay in the family room with his older brothers. However, if he touched their handiwork in any way, he would be confined to his own bedroom until Ben and Matthew were finished playing with the blocks. The choice was his: obedience or confinement. More often than not he had to be confined!

Now let me ask a question. Which was greater proof of my love for my children: to allow the evil and suffering (tower destruction, in this case, and the annoyance it caused) to continue with no consequence, or to remove the perpetrator of the problem and confine him? If I allowed Jonathan to remain in the family room and wreak havoc, *none* of you would have experienced any joy. Very soon there would have been disruption, dismay, anger, and distress — and quite possibly some pain. (You grew quite perturbed!) However, if I removed him the rest of you could experience peace, pleasure, harmony, and joy as you played happily together.

Was it my fault that Jonathan had to be separated from his older brothers and confined in his room? No. It was the consequence of his own choice.

God does not choose to ignore those who reject Him. Because of His love, He chooses to confine them. Hell is a place of confinement (distantly analogous to Jonathan's bedroom!). Just as a place of incarceration was necessary to keep tranquility in our home, hell's existence is necessary if there is to be peace and joy in God's kingdom. And just as it wasn't my choice to send Jonathan to his room, it isn't God's choice to send people to hell. Second Peter 3:9 tells us that God is "not wanting anyone to perish, but everyone to come to repentance." It would be His greatest joy for every single human being to join Him in heaven someday. But people assign themselves to hell by rejecting His offer of salvation and restoration.

Hell is a place that displays God's love just as much as it demonstrates His justice. Let me say that again just in case you read over it too quickly. *Hell is a place that displays God's love just as much as it demonstrates His justice.* If God allowed everyone to enter heaven regardless of their sin (as some people believe He does), very soon we would find ourselves living under worse circumstances than we already have here on earth.

Suppose a gunman sneaked his way onto your school campus and began to spray bullets into the classrooms, injuring and killing several students. After they captured him, what do you think would be the appropriate and most loving course of action for the police to take? Should they just talk to him for a while, then let him go, or should they confine him to a place where he can do no further harm to society?

You know the answer. It's obvious. You see, justice is not the only criterion that demands confinement of criminals. So does love.

But why doesn't God just completely annihilate the people who choose to reject Him? When He figures they've spent enough time here on earth, why doesn't He just zap them into oblivion? That would do away with the problem of allowing any sin into heaven to corrupt it and cause chaos.

This solution creates several problems. First, when Jesus took our sins with Him to the cross, He had to experience both physical death (cessation of life) and spiritual death (separation from God). If the spiritual death He suffered on our behalf led to the annihilation of His soul, then no resurrection would have been possible. Annihilation, by its very definition, has to be permanent. If Jesus had been annihilated, there would have been no body, soul, or spirit to be resurrected. Yet, as we studied in answering Question #4, the Resurrection is the foundation on which all of Christianity is based. None of us could go to heaven if Jesus had not been raised from the dead!

The Bible describes hell as a very real place, a place set apart for the confinement of all sin and evil. As a matter of fact, Jesus taught more about this place called hell than He did about heaven. Twelve times the word *gehenna* (the strongest word for hell) is used in the New Testament. Eleven of those times it came from the mouth of Jesus. Of the forty parables Jesus told, more than half relate to God's eternal judgment on sin. Jesus describes hell as a place of fire (see Matthew 5:22; 25:41), darkness and weeping (see Matthew 8:12; 25:30), eternal punishment (see Matthew 25:46), and unending misery (see Mark 9:43-48). He describes it as a place for those who reject Him (see Matthew 13:41-43). To claim that there is no existence after death for those who reject God is to call Jesus Christ a liar.

One more problem with the speculation that God could choose immediately to annihilate those who do not accept His loving offer is the fact that annihilation avoids the concept of punishment. John Gerstner (one of the premier theologians of the twentieth century) said, "One can exist and not be punished, but no one can be punished and not exist."[1] You see, annihilation means the obliteration of existence. You can't be punished if you don't exist. Therefore, there would be no real consequence to sinning. What a horrible planet this would be if no one on it feared the eternal consequences of his or her actions!

The only loving option God had available was to confine those who choose to reject Him in a place devoid of His presence, a place we call hell. And that is exactly what the Bible teaches us He did.

Theologians have argued for years over whether or not the fire and agony that Jesus and others in the Bible mention when they describe hell are literal (actually real) or figurative (just a way of expressing a concept). But I don't think it really matters. Just the fact that there will not be a single ray or even a reflection of God's holiness in hell makes it a place of tragedy and despair beyond anything we can imagine.

You see, hell is the necessary consequence of man's rebellion and rejection. And only by accepting the existence of hell can we grasp the overwhelming immensity of God's love. It was a costly love that took His only Son to a bloody, cruel cross in our place. It is a love that pursues us, woos us, and even begs us to accept it. But because it *is* love, it does not force itself upon us.

In the early 1920s, Calvin Coolidge was vice president of the United States. One of his jobs was to preside over the Senate. One day two of the senators got into a heated debate. Finally, one of them stood up and very angrily told the other to "go straight to hell." The offended senator was very upset and complained to Coolidge, demanding that he make some kind of ruling. Coolidge looked up from the Bible he had been paging through while the debate was going on. "I've been looking through the rule book," he responded with his dry sense of humor, "and you don't *have* to go!"

No one *has* to go to hell. The choice is ours. Do we want to spend our eternity suffering the agony and regret of hell or basking in the joy and satisfaction of heaven?

THE JOY OF HEAVEN

The Bible teaches us that heaven is the holy habitation of God (see 1 Kings 8:30; Psalm 103:19). It was Christ's perfect home before He came to earth (see John 6:38), the place He joyfully returned to when He left (see Luke 24:51), and where He lives now (see Hebrews 8:1-2). And most significantly for us, heaven is the place God has assigned Jesus to prepare for those who accept His loving gift of pardon (see John 14:2-3). We can't even begin to imagine the splendor and joy of living in His presence for all eternity!

Picture yourself relaxing in the most perfect place on this planet on the most perfect day possible. Perhaps it's a sandy beach gently caressed by shimmering, blue water and a soft ocean breeze. Or maybe you're on a snow-covered mountaintop overlooking a valley filled with emerald-green pines and a crystal-clear lake reflecting a bright blue sky with puffy white clouds. Whatever you can best envision on your most imaginative day — no matter how perfect it seems — is flawed. That's because everything in creation has been tainted by the world's sinfulness. *But everything will be perfect in heaven!* Try to imagine God's creative genius revealed in all its perfection. It's impossible. First Corinthians 2:9 puts it this way: "No eye has seen, no ear has heard, no mind has conceived what God has prepared for those who love him."

Peter Kreeft, after studying the last two chapters in the book of Revelation, describes heaven as:

a city shining like a precious stone, clear as crystal. Its wall is made of jasper and its foundations are adorned with precious stones. Its twelve gates are made of pearl and its streets of pure gold. The glory of God lights this city, and nothing impure is found in it. The river of the water of life flows from the throne of God, and on each side of the river is a tree of life, the leaves of which are for the healing of the nations. Whatever Heaven is, it is God's plan for us, and God is very wise, very good, very loving, and very full of surprises.[2]

In heaven there will be no illness, no death, no arguments, no dads packing suitcases to go on long business trips or moms threatening to move out to find a better life. Our friends won't live in nicer houses or go on better vacations or tease us because of our big ears. There will be no homeless people or war-ravaged countries, no crime, no tears, no darkness, no fears. Heaven will be a place of pure joy, and the focus of our joy will be God. We will forget about our own needs because we won't have any! There will be no pride or despair, no anger or boredom. It is where we will live forever enjoying perfect relationships in the presence of God — if we choose to accept God's loving way out of the debt we owe for our sins.

SUMMARY

In order to enjoy true love from His created beings, God formed them with the ability to make choices. All choices have consequences. When Adam and Eve chose to reject God, they chose to plunge all of mankind into sin and therefore separate us from our holy God. God lovingly sent His Son to die in our place and pay our penalty of separation. Jesus willingly exchanged His righteousness for our sin on the cross.

Now each individual has a choice to make: to accept or reject God's loving offer of forgiveness and pardon. If we reject God, we choose to endure the consequence of sin— separation from His presence. We cannot enter heaven, because our sin would contaminate His pure holiness. We cannot be annihilated because that would negate the consequences of our choice and make Jesus a liar. So we must be confined away from His presence. That place of confinement is called hell. It is a place devoid of holiness, home to only tragedy and despair.

But if we accept God's offer to enjoy a relationship with Him through what Jesus Christ did in our place, we are free to enter an eternity of happiness and joy. We are invited to join Him in heaven, a place far more perfect than anything we could ever imagine!

The choice is ours!

ONE MORE THING

I almost forgot to tell you what happened to the man I mentioned at the beginning of the chapter — the game-show contestant who had to make an important choice about money. Well, he turned his swivel chair around, accepted a check, and walked off the stage with $125,000 in his pocket. He decided to take the escape option he had been offered rather than risk losing everything. What a smart man! What a wise decision! As it turned out, he would have missed the next question anyway. That would have been a tragedy — but *nothing* compared to the tragedy of an eternity separated from God!

In a sense, God wants to hand you the biggest check you could ever receive, a check that will pay off all the debt of your sin and allow you to live in His presence forever. Don't risk losing it! Accept His offer today before it is too late. Once we die we don't get another chance (see Hebrews 9:27)!

QUESTION #10

WHAT DOES IT MEAN
to Believe?

CHRISTMAS MORNINGS USED TO START DARK AND EARLY AT OUR HOUSE. The sun was still fast asleep when a whole herd of kids pounded their way down our stairs, racing faster than little feet should be able to fly. All four of you would burst into the living room and start jumping up and down and squealing at the sight of presents that had been stacked haphazardly around the tree the night before. (We didn't dare put them out any earlier, knowing that no secrets would remain on Christmas morning!)

In an effort to maintain some semblance of order, the gifts were distributed one at a time. Everyone had to wait patiently as each recipient ripped off paper, shrieked with joy, and passed the gift for all to see. Hugs and kisses were abundant. When Mrs. Horn lived next door, you would tear across the yard to show her your new treasures. No one loved to share in your joy as much as Mrs. Horn!

But one Christmas morning, in the midst of all the excitement and unwrapping and screaming and running next door, I was left holding a wrapped gift in my hands. It was a relatively small one labeled "To Matthew." He had placed it in my safekeeping until he could open all his larger ones. I held it . . . and held it . . . and held it, as he unwrapped one gift after another. He often checked to make sure I still had it, but MattE never made any effort to retrieve it. He was too occupied with bigger, brighter gifts under the tree. I think he finally forgot about it. Little did he know that I was holding the gift he wanted most — a new remote-controlled racing car!

After unwrapping all the gifts that were labeled for him, Jonathan spied the gift in my hands. He reached over and grabbed it. "If MattE doesn't want it, I do!" he exclaimed as he tore off the bow, ripping the paper and revealing the box of a much-desired car. It became the focus of everyone's attention for most of the day.

That gift was of no value to Matthew, or anyone else, while it sat unopened in my hands. It wasn't until Jonathan grabbed it and began to unwrap it that the present took on any meaning and provided any pleasure in anyone's life. (I recall a little pain it brought as well, as Matthew extricated it from Jonathan's grip — but that's beside the point!)

God has a gift — the payment for our sins through the death of His Son Jesus. His arms are extended as He offers it to each one of us. He holds it . . . and holds it . . . and holds it, making it available to us. We just need to accept the gift and it will be ours. John 3:16 says, "For God so loved the world that he gave his one and only Son, that whoever believes in him shall not perish but have eternal life."

But what on earth does it mean "to believe"? Here is a story that might help us understand.

When all four of you were small, you used to run into the backyard each time you heard an airplane go overhead. Some of them flew very low over our house since there was a small airport nearby. As a matter of fact, each spring that airport sponsored a huge fly-in, and all kinds of airplanes from all over the country flew directly over our roof. You used to love to climb the tree in the backyard (and sometimes even onto the roof!) to watch the air-show acrobatics, the brightly decorated hot-air balloons, and the strangely shaped ultralite machines from your special vantage point.

Airplanes were a source of great mystery and fascination. We borrowed books from the library so that you could begin to understand aerodynamics and how flight took place. You bought model airplanes and hung them from your ceilings. We crawled all through gigantic rescue helicopters at a special Coast Guard show and visited the big science museum to check out exhibits about aviation.

During those years, Dad traveled a lot, and often we dropped him off at the little airport nearby to catch a commuter plane to Tampa or Orlando. We said goodbye to him at the tiny terminal, then parked the car where we could watch his plane take off. We sat on the tailgate of our big old station wagon, or on the roof, and waved until his plane was out of sight. Ben was about three years old and, although he was usually one of the rowdier kids in the family, he always became very quiet and introspective when we arrived at the airport. He stared, with his lips sealed shut and his eyes wide open, as the plane took off in the distance. Then he rode home silently in the back seat of the car. When I asked what was bothering him, he never responded. Once in a while he asked strange questions like, "Will Daddy be big when he comes home?" or "Does Daddy get hurt in the airplane?"

After we arrived home, he would turn into a wild child again — until it was time to return to the airport to pick up Dad. Then once again he became quiet. He was a little statue until Dad stepped off the plane. Then Ben would run to greet him, throw himself into Dad's arms, and say something like "Daddy's big."

"Yep, Daddy's big," we would repeat, wondering why size was suddenly so important.

Then came a special day when we all got to go to the big airport in Tampa to fly to Dallas. Ben kept asking strange questions as we packed, like "Will my clothes still fit me in the airplane?" On the way to the airport he wanted to know, "Does it hurt to be little?" We answered as best we could, sometimes shrugging our shoulders or shaking our heads.

Ben walked like a zombie through the terminal and silently tiptoed beside me to the gate. Everyone was exuberant when they called for us to board — everyone except Ben. He clung to my hand, his face ashen. He hesitated as we were about to step from the ramp onto the plane, but clutching me with one hand and his little backpack with the other, he followed me to our seats. We arranged and rearranged our seating assignments, jockeying for the best window or aisle seats. Ben just sat quietly. We got out our favorite toys and snacks. Ben stared out the window. I buckled his seatbelt for takeoff. Ben gripped the armrests. "Here we go — now we're in the air!" someone narrated from beside him. Ben sat as still as a stone.

About five minutes after takeoff Ben reached over and tugged on my sleeve. "Mommy, when do we get little?" he whispered. I was obviously puzzled. "You know," he tried to explain, "like Daddy does when he gets on an airplane and it goes in the sky. He gets real little! When does that happen to us?"

Suddenly it all made sense. For the first time I understood Ben's airport dilemma. When it came to watching airplanes he had no clue about depth perception. As they disappeared into the horizon, he thought they were shrinking. He obviously thought he was about to be reduced to the size of a mosquito!

It took awhile, but Ben finally caught on to the concept of living in a three-dimensional world. But I told you that story for a purpose. I want to use it to illustrate what the Bible means when it tells us we have to "believe" in order to receive God's gift of eternal life.

BELIEF GOES BEYOND INTELLECTUAL ASSENT

When the Bible was first translated from Greek into Latin, three different words were used to describe three different levels of belief. These three expressions were translated into the English language as the words "believe" or "receive." However, if we study the three different Latin terms, we can begin to understand the biblical concept of belief a lot better.

If anyone had asked you guys during your childhood years if you believed that airplanes could fly, you would have looked at him as if he were stupid. "Of course we believe airplanes can fly," you would have said. "We see them fly over our house every day."

When you observed the airplanes going overhead in the back-yard, you *noticed* that they were in the air, therefore you *believed* that they could fly. The Latin word *noticia* would be used to describe this type of belief. It is the belief that comes from objec-tively observing the facts.

But when we went to the library and borrowed books about air-planes and visited aviation displays at the museum you began to understand the academics supporting aerodynamics. At that point you could *assentia* that airplanes fly. Not only did you believe based on your own observations, you could *intellectually assent* (agree) that it was physically possible for those big machines to get off the ground and fly like birds. Your belief was no longer based merely on objective facts. You believed that airplanes could fly based on intellectual knowledge.

But only when you stepped on board the airplane in Tampa did you believe in the sense that the Bible uses the word. The Latin word is *fiducia* and it means to "receive the solution personally." It means that you are willing to put the facts you have noticed and the knowledge you have accumulated to the test. It means that you are willing to trust your life to those facts and that knowledge — just as we trusted our lives to that big airplane that claimed it could take us to Dallas. I have to admit, Ben's faith was a lot more tentative, and therefore a lot more dramatic, than the rest of ours! For him to step aboard that airplane and entrust his life to that pilot required great *fiducia!*

As you have read this book, you have *noticed* many *facts*. You have noticed that the existence of God is evident throughout nature. You may have noticed that one of the biggest differences between Christianity and other world religions is that Christianity is based on a God who reaches down to man, while all other religions force man to try to find his own way up to God. You probably noticed that several men who sought to discredit Christianity found themselves accepting it as truth. Believing these facts is not enough.

Hopefully, after studying this book you have come to an *intellectual understanding* that it is more intelligent to accept the fact that there is a God than to deny His existence. You have learned there is ample evidence to back up the fact that the Bible is a reliable document and even more evidence to prove that the resurrection of Jesus Christ actually took place. You may even have acknowledged intellectually that everything you have read makes sense and is probably correct. You may believe that God loves us and wants to provide a way for us (even though we are sinful) to enter His holy presence and live in joy with Him for eternity. But this is not enough.

Noticing the facts *(noticia)* and accepting them intellectually *(assentia)* is not the type of "belief" or "receiving" talked about in John 3:16 (or John 1:12; Acts 16:31; 1 Corinthians 15:1-3; Colossians 2:6). Only when you are willing to trust your life to what God has promised, and are ready to let go of everything else that you have previously put your confidence in, do you truly *believe (fiducia)* in the biblical sense. It's like stepping on board that airplane and trusting it to take you where it has promised it would. Here is another example that might make this clearer.

BELIEF INVOLVES PERSONAL TRUST

Not long ago the History Channel featured a special about Niagara Falls. It focused on the story of Jean Francois Gravelet, known as "The Great Blondin," who crossed the Niagara gorge several times on a tightrope during the summer of 1859. His dangerous high-wire act drew crowds of up to 25,000 people.

With the help of his manager, Blondin would explain to the crowds that gathered what he was about to do. Together they would incite the mass of onlookers into boisterous cheering by asking if they believed The Great Blondin could make it across. "We believe! We believe!" they would yell. Blondin would then proceed to cross holding onto a long balancing pole.

One time he went even further. "Do you believe I can cross the Falls on this wire pushing a wheelbarrow?" he challenged the cheering mob. "Yes, we believe!" they screamed in response.

Blondin precariously guided the wheelbarrow (and himself!) safely across the great chasm. But he wasn't finished.

"Do you believe that I can cross the Falls on this wire pushing a wheelbarrow with a grown man inside?" he questioned. "Do it!" they bellowed. "We believe!" The crowd was excited to a frenzy.

"Then who will go first?" Blondin asked.

Absolute silence. No one dared holler back or raise his hand.

As the story goes, Blondin finally leaned over and whispered something in his manager's ear. The manager crawled onto Blondin's back (somehow he must have felt that he was a little safer connected to Blondin than stuck in a wheelbarrow), and Blondin carried him across the great gorge to the other side.

The only one who truly believed that Blondin could make it across Niagara Falls carrying the weight of another person was the manager. His belief went beyond intellectual assent to personal trust. He was willing to put his faith completely in what he had observed and what he had acknowledged that Blondin could do.

This type of belief requires a decision, a choice to be made. Unfortunately we often define belief or faith as the absence of doubt. That is not true. It is a decision based on the evidence we have. It is choosing to put our observations and knowledge into action even when we don't have all the answers. Belief does not require a certain level of faith. When we stepped on board that airplane in Tampa, I dare say that Ben had very little faith that it would actually get him to Dallas (at least not without squishing him to the size of a pea!). But the fact that he had minimal faith did not mean that the airplane was any less capable of getting him there. He arrived just as safely and promptly as the rest of us did.

Dr. David DeWitt, in his book *Answering the Tough Ones*, tells a story that illustrates this point:

> Once while discussing (faith) at a lunch with a man, I
> poured some coffee out of my cup onto the table just in
> front of him. Then I asked him if he believed the napkin
> I was holding could wipe it up before it ran onto his
> pants. He sat for a moment watching the spill get closer
> and closer to his lap, then answered, "No — yes — I don't

know — give me that thing!" Then he grabbed the napkin and wiped up the stream of coffee before it spilled off the table onto his suit. I then explained how, of the four responses he made, three of them ("yes," "no," and "I don't know") were all useless faith. To respond, "Yes," to Christ is just as useless as to respond "No," or, "I don't know," if it does not involve receiving Him. The Bible says, "The demons also believe, and shudder" (James 2:19). The spilled coffee made clear to him that only when he received Christ like he received the napkin would his sins be wiped away.[1]

You have a decision to make. Do you want to receive God's wonderful gift of eternal life or not? If so, just let Him know that you believe — that you personally trust His solution for your sin problem. Talk to God and say something like this:

I know that I am a sinner and that my sin separates me from You. I know that I cannot reach You or live up to Your holy standards on my own. I believe that You sent Jesus to this earth, that He lived a sinless life, and that He paid the penalty for all my sins when He died on the cross. But I also know that He rose from the dead! And I want to place my trust in Him as my Savior. Today I am going to start living my life on the basis of the promises and plans You have for me in the Bible. Thank You for loving and forgiving me and giving me the gift of eternal life. In Jesus' name, Amen.

There is no greater gift that you can ever receive than the gift you just accepted if you prayed that prayer!

SUMMARY

To believe in Christ means to notice and understand intellectually that your sin separates you from God's holiness. There is no way on your own that you can ever come into His presence. It's as if there is a great chasm between you and God. But God, in His holiness and love, has provided a way to bridge that chasm. He sent His only Son, Jesus, to take your place. He died on the cross and suffered not only physical death, but spiritual death (separation from God) so that you don't have to. But noticing and understanding this is not enough. Belief must go beyond factual knowledge and intellectual assent. It must become personal trust. In a sense you must get on Jesus' back and allow Him to do what only He can do, and that is carry you across the chasm into God's presence. You must transfer your trust from anything you could do for yourself to what Jesus Christ has already done for you.

It's like that Christmas present we talked about at the beginning of this chapter. If I had been God and that gift I had for Matthew had been eternal life, the only one who would have enjoyed a lifetime in heaven would have been Jonathan. Instead of just looking at the pretty package, he reached out and grabbed it from me.

God has the most tremendous gift we could ever imagine for us. His arms are extended. He is holding it . . . and holding it . . . and holding it! All we have to do is accept the gift — doubts and all. John 1:12 says, "To all who *received* him, to those who *believed* in his name, he gave the right to become children of God" (emphasis mine). Wow! We're not merely invited to enter God's presence. We are invited to be His children! We're going to be treated as princes and princesses. How awesome! Can you even imagine being a child of the King of the universe!

QUESTION #11

CAN I BE SURE I'M
Going to Heaven?

MANY YEARS AGO WE LIVED IN A LITTLE TOWN OUTSIDE PORTLAND, Oregon. While there, Dad helped start a seminar ministry called Walk Thru the Bible. The early days included a lot of travel across the nation as the seminars became more and more popular. Soon the organization decided it would be much more efficient if it were located in a large city with an international airport. So it was announced that everyone in the company would be moving to Atlanta the next summer. I'll never forget how surprised I was when Dad shared this news with me!

Several months before the move, Dad began making trips to Georgia to find us a place to live. He spent days scouring the city and searching the suburbs for just the right location. He finally settled on a wonderful, tree-shaded lot and set the plans in motion to begin building our dream house. He chose colors and patterns (with a little input from me!). He made arrangements to move our furniture. He checked out schools and parks, and found a nice church.

He made all the plans he possibly could ahead of time so that when we arrived everything would be wonderfully smooth and simple.

Never once did we doubt that Dad would come back to get us, because he always promised he would. All along we knew that the reason he left was to prepare a place for us. We understood that sometime soon he would take us back to live with him there.

Sure enough, the day finally arrived when we all flew to Atlanta and (after a few hassles with the builders) moved into our wonderful new home in Peachtree City, Georgia!

JESUS PROMISED TO PREPARE US A PLACE

John 14 tells us about the day when Jesus told His disciples that it was time for Him to leave this world and go to be with His Father in heaven. His friends seemed startled and began to question Him about His decision. This is what He told them:

> "Do not let your hearts be troubled. Trust in God; trust also in me. In my Father's house are many rooms; if it were not so, I would have told you. I am going there to prepare a place for you. And if I go and prepare a place for you, I will come back and take you to be with me that you also may be where I am. You know the way to the place where I am going." (John 14:1-4)

I can just imagine the disciples looking around at each other and whispering, "Do you know what He's talking about?" "I don't have a clue where He's going." "Do you know how to get to His Father's house, because *I* sure don't know how to get to His Father's house?" "Why hasn't He taken us there before?" But no one dared to say anything — except Thomas, who finally blurted out, "Lord, we don't know where you are going, so how can we know the way?" (verse 5).

I'm not sure if Thomas wanted Jesus to get out a map and show him the route, or draw him a set of directions on a piece of papyrus, or just give him instructions like you would if your friends were coming to our house for a party. ("Take the second left after the lake and it's the third house on the right — the big gray one with the baseball flag out front.") But Jesus simply replied, "I am the way and the truth and the life. No one comes to the Father except through me" (verse 6).

You see, the way to heaven isn't found by motoring along some superhighway, or meandering across a winding path, or detouring down a hidden alley. It's found in a person — the person of Jesus Christ. He came to earth to provide us with a way — the *only* way — to heaven. And when we *believe* (the word we studied in the last chapter) that Jesus' death on the cross was the payment for our sins, we are invited to join Him forever in heaven.

But here's the best part of the story. When Jesus left this earth, He didn't just go back to heaven to be with His Father. He had a job to do. At this very moment He is preparing a place for us in heaven. (If I think about this for very long it blows my mind. Can you picture Jesus picking out wallpaper for your room? And if God created everything on this planet in just seven days like it says in the book of Genesis, can you even begin to imagine what kind of place will be prepared for us after 2,000 years of His creativity!)

Jesus *promised* that when everything is ready He *will* come back to get us and take us to be with Him forever. Never once has any promise in the Bible been broken. This one won't be, either!

That means that if we have prayed a prayer similar to the one at the end of Question #10, we will one day live in heaven in the most awesome housing development — wait a minute, let's make that resort — we can ever imagine!

But what if we sin — maybe even a lot — after we accept God's gift of salvation? Will we still get to go to heaven? Or what if we doubt so much that soon we wonder if we still believe at all? These are great questions, and God has great answers.

GOD PROMISED TO PROTECT US WHILE WE WAIT

Each one of you burst into this world in your own unique way. Zach rushed onto the scene several weeks earlier than the doctor had predicted and caused quite a stir with his premature appearance. Matthew moseyed in right on schedule and took charge of life from day one. Ben held off until Mama's stomach could not manage one more centimeter of growth. And Jonathan, not wanting to be rushed, waited for the doctor to take a much-needed break before he decided it was the perfect moment to arrive.

But each of you had one thing in common. You came into the world as part of our family. From the moment you were conceived you were our child, and we were your parents. Nothing you did on the way into this world changed that fact. Nothing you have done since has altered that relationship. Nothing you will ever do can sever that bond. No matter what happens, the fact remains that you will always be our child.

If you choose to be compliant and obey, you are our child. If you choose to be rebellious and disobey, you are still our child. If you choose to have a pet tarantula, or paint your bedroom silver with black polka dots, or fill your brother's shoes with shaving cream, or sneak out of the house at midnight to buy Slurpees with your friends and then hate us when we ground you — no matter what you do — you will always be our child!

You see, our relationship does not change based on what you do or don't do. It is permanent. What changes is our fellowship. You might get pretty tired of our rules and regulations, and we might get pretty perturbed with your responses. At times conversations and situations may become rather intense or uncomfortable. But the fact that we have a relationship as parent and child will never change. The only thing that fluctuates is the camaraderie — the fellowship — we are able to enjoy.

We have already seen that God has offered a wonderful gift — the gift of eternal life in heaven — to everyone who personally trusts Christ for his/her salvation. But He has promised something else. At the end of Question #10 we quoted John 1:12: "To all who *received* him, to those who *believed* in his name, he gave the right to become *children of God*" (emphasis mine).

If you have personally trusted the fact that Jesus' death on the cross was God's way of allowing you to enter into His glorious, holy presence, then you not only have eternal life — you are a child of God. God is your Father! And nothing can ever change that relationship — *nothing* that you think, *nothing* that you do, *nothing* that you say!

Think about it this way. When you were little, you used to cling to Dad's hand as you walked down to the lake behind our house. Fortunately, your safety didn't depend on *your* grip — as five of your little fingers clutched one of his. Your safety depended on the fact that Dad wrapped his big hand around yours. Often you slipped on wet leaves or stumbled over the rocks. Sometimes you lifted up your legs and swung from his hand on purpose. And just about every time the walk was over and Dad started to head home, you tried to get away. But he didn't let you go. He knew that in less than five seconds you'd be in that water. He knew how quickly you could disappear into its murky depths and how incapable you were of climbing back up the slippery bank.

The same is true of God. He clings onto His children as they walk through life. Listen to what Jesus said:

"I give them eternal life, and they shall never perish; no one can snatch them out of my hand. My Father, who has given them to me, is greater than all; no one can snatch them out of my Father's hand." (John 10:28-29)

Our heavenly Father doesn't always keep us from stumbling. He doesn't prevent us from rebelling. But He never lets go of our hand. He never allows us to be removed from our relationship with Him. One of my favorite Bible passages is Romans 8. Verse 35 asks this question:

Who shall separate us from the love of Christ? Shall trouble or hardship or persecution or famine or nakedness or danger or sword?

Verses 38-39 reply:

For I am convinced that neither death nor life, neither angels nor demons, neither the present nor the future, nor any powers, neither height nor depth, (I can just picture Paul running out of opposite extremes to use here. He probably spread his arms, shook his head and added in a loud, wonderfully Jewish accent) nor *anything* else in all creation, will be able to separate us from the love of God that is in Christ Jesus our Lord (emphasis mine).

Wow! Talk about being safe. Once we are children of God, *nothing* can separate us from Him!

At times we will have doubts, and at times we will sin — but once we enter God's family we will always be His children. That's because the relationship doesn't depend on us. It depends on God! When Jesus died on the cross for the sins of the whole world (see 1 John 2:2), He died for all of them — past, present, and future. He paid for *all* of the sins of *all* the people for *all* time. How many of our sins were still in the future when Christ died 2,000 years ago? All of them, right? So His sacrifice will have no problem covering any more sins we might commit. Sure, when we sin it hurts God tremendously (see Ephesians 4:30-31). It causes us pain, too, (see Proverbs 5:22) and we lose some of the rewards we could have received in heaven (see 1 Timothy 5:24-25). But our sins and our doubts cannot separate us from God. They cannot make His eternal gift to us invalid.

THE BIBLE PROMISES THAT IT WILL LAST FOREVER

Shortly after we moved from Georgia to Florida, we were determined to buy a swing set for the backyard. With four active kids it would have to be a good and sturdy one. We knew that a small aluminum model couldn't stand up to the wear and tear it would receive on a daily basis. So we saved our money and invested in a large wooden contraption that we ordered from a catalog. It came with a lifetime warranty. Can't beat that, right?

The swing set was manufactured in New England. Little did they know that wood that lasted for centuries up North would deteriorate rapidly in the humid climate, searing sunlight, and swarming bug infestations of central Florida. Piece by piece we began to send parts of the swing set back to be replaced. And piece by piece new parts were shipped to us in return. If we had added it all up, we probably replaced the entire swing set three or four different times! The company finally realized that they were losing money, so they made a cash offer to buy us out of the warranty. We agreed and tore the thing down and used it for firewood.

We found out that a lifetime warranty made by human beings sometimes has its limits. But not so with God!

You may have noticed that sometimes I refer to one of the gifts we receive from God as "salvation." Some people call it being "born again." But it is most often referred to in the Bible as "eternal life." At least fifty-two times in the Bible God uses the word *eternal* — *aionios* in Greek — to describe the gift He offers to us. *Aionios* means "eternal, forever, everlasting," and (I really like this phrase) — "since the world began without end."[1] Of all the major world religions, biblical Christianity is the only one that teaches that we cannot lose our salvation. Every other system requires human effort to "hold on." It is dependent on each individual to maintain a lifestyle worthy of that religion's reward.

Some Christians argue that a number of Bible verses indicate that we *can* lose our salvation. However when we look closely at these verses, none of them really conflicts with what the rest of Scripture teaches so clearly — that salvation and eternal life cannot be taken away for any reason. More often than not, these passages aren't referring to salvation at all, but to growth and maturity as a believer. If God knew our salvation was something we could lose, He certainly wouldn't have used the word *eternal* to describe it so many times. Here are just a few of the wonderful verses promising that our trip to live with Him in heaven will last forever (emphasis mine throughout):

> For God so loved the world that he gave his one and only Son, that whoever believes in him shall not perish but have *eternal* life. (John 3:16)

"I tell you the truth, whoever hears my word and believes him who sent me has *eternal* life and will not be condemned; he has crossed over from death to life." (John 5:24)

"I give them *eternal* life, and they shall never perish; no one can snatch them out of my hand." (John 10:28)

For the wages of sin is death, but the gift of God is *eternal* life in Christ Jesus our Lord. (Romans 6:23)

And this is what he promised us — even *eternal* life. (1 John 2:25)

God has given us *eternal* life, and this life is in His Son. (1 John 5:11)

There's one more verse I must share with you because it makes God's intent so evident. Wanting to assure us that God's gift of eternal life can never be taken away, John writes this to believers struggling with the very same question: "I write these things to you who believe in the name of the Son of God so that you may **KNOW** that you have *eternal* life" (1 John 5:13, emphasis mine).

God doesn't want us to wonder if we're going to spend eternity in heaven with Him. He wants us to know beyond a shadow of a doubt that when we accept His sacrificial gift of love, we will live with Him forever and ever in the joy and peace and perfection of heaven!

I'm so excited that I will be spending eternity in heaven with you! I can't wait to see the rooms that Jesus has prepared for you!

SUMMARY

A home is being prepared for us right now, a place for us to spend the rest of eternity. It will be magnificent beyond anything we can imagine. Heaven is a place of complete beauty, joy, peace, and pleasure!

Meanwhile God, our Father, holds our hands as we walk along the slippery path of life. He never lets us out of His grip for even an instant. No matter how much we doubt or even sin, He will not let go of us. God is the one responsible for securing our relationship. The status of our fellowship, however, is up to us. We will study more about that in our next book.

Your position as God's child will never change or come to an end. He has promised you that His gifts of love and life will last for all eternity! Yes, you can be sure you're going to heaven!

DISCUSSION QUESTIONS

QUESTION #1: CAN YOU PROVE TO ME THAT THERE IS A GOD?

1. Read Psalm 19:1-4 and Romans 1:18-20. In what ways has God revealed Himself through His creation?

2. What can you know about God's personality by observing His creation?

3. Do you remember a specific time when you felt drawn to God through His creation?

4. Name a virtue or moral standard that has been universally accepted. Describe different ways that different cultures have shown that they accept it as a standard. How does this indicate the existence of God?

5. Can you think of a recent discovery or scientific experiment that points to the existence of a Power beyond our knowledge and understanding?

6. Summarize the five arguments that provide evidence for the existence of an eternal, intelligent, ethical, and personal God:

   a. The argument of sufficient cause:

   b. The argument of motion:

   c. The argument of design:

   d. The argument of morality:

   e. The argument of personality:

QUESTION #2: IF THERE IS A GOD, WHY DOES HE ALLOW SO
MUCH SUFFERING?

1. What do evil and rust have in common?
2. Why did God create us with the option to choose good or evil? Why didn't He make us capable of only choosing good?
2. What is the difference between moral evil and natural evil? How did they both come into existence?
3. Describe some of the ways that the evil choice Adam and Eve made affects your life. What are some forms of "suffering" that you are experiencing right now?
4. If God is all-loving and all-powerful, why does He allow pain and suffering to continue?
5. Read 2 Peter 3:7-12. Should knowing that God will one day destroy all evil affect the way you live your life today? How?

QUESTION #3: HOW DO WE KNOW THAT THE BIBLE IS A
RELIABLE SOURCE?

1. How has archaeology helped prove the reliability of the Bible?
2. Read Ezekiel 26. (It was written in 586 B.C.) How does the fact that King Nebuchadnezzar began a fifteen-year siege against Tyre later that year and that Alexander the Great destroyed the city completely in 332 B.C. help validate the Bible as a document?
3. How does the unified theme of the Bible point to its authenticity?
4. How do the early Bible manuscripts measure up to those written by Plato and Aristotle that we also accept as authentic?
5. How did godly men meeting at the Council of Hippo in A.D. 397 determine which books belonged in the Bible?
6. What one simple question should we ask ourselves when inter-

preting a Bible passage? How does this do away with most of the questions we will have concerning interpretation?

7. What difference does it make in your life whether or not the Bible is a reliable document?

QUESTION #4: DID THE MIRACLES IN THE BIBLE REALLY
HAPPEN?

1. What is the difference between a "wonder of nature" and a "miracle"?

2. How do scientific laws and miracles relate to each other?

3. Explain the statement made on page 57: "If you rule out miracles, you rule out God and Christianity completely."

4. Read Matthew 12:22-24. Why did the Pharisees and Sadducees only challenge Jesus' *source* of power or His *right to perform* miracles rather than the fact that He actually performed them?

5. Respond to the following "explanations" that deny the miracle of the resurrection of Jesus Christ:

   a. Due to their grief, Jesus' disciples mistakenly went to the wrong tomb.

   b. Jesus' followers wanted Him to be alive SO much that they hallucinated His appearances to them after His death.

   c. Jesus' disciples concocted a scheme to spread a false story of the Resurrection.

6. What difference does it make to you whether or not the Resurrection took place?

QUESTION #5: ISN'T IT NARROW-MINDED TO SAY THAT JESUS
IS THE ONLY WAY TO GOD?

1. Describe some instance when being narrow-minded is better than being open-minded or tolerant.

2. Explain the statement: "Truth is always narrow."

3. Describe a time in history when the majority of people in a society upheld a belief that was not true. Did the society's opinion make it true? How was it proven wrong?

4. Can you name a time when you or a friend sincerely believed that something was true, but later found out that it was not? Did your sincerity affect the truth of the situation?

5. How does Jesus' statement in John 14:6 disagree with claims that He was merely a good man, a wise leader, or a great moral teacher?

6. Based on this claim, what are the only three options we have concerning Jesus' true identity?

7. If we accept Jesus' claim that He is the only way to heaven as true, how should it affect our relationships with others?

QUESTION #6: WHAT ABOUT THOSE WHO HAVE NEVER HEARD ABOUT JESUS?

1. According to Romans 1:19-20 and Romans 2:15, what are the two ways God reveals Himself to people who haven't heard the gospel message?

2. How do the standards that we set for ourselves and our consciences make us aware of a Superior Being?

3. According to 1 Chronicles 28:9, what is God's obligation to a person who accepts His existence yet has not heard the gospel message?

4. How did God miraculously fulfill this obligation in the life of the Ethiopian eunuch (see Acts 8:26-39)?

5. Can you think of another time (in the Bible or more recently) when God revealed the message of Jesus Christ in a unique and powerful way?

6. Read Acts 1:8 and 1 Peter 3:15. According to these verses, what is our role in bringing God's message to those who have never heard?

QUESTION #7: ISN'T LIVING A GOOD LIFE GOOD ENOUGH?

1. According to Matthew 5:43-48, what standard does God require us to reach before we can become His children and enter heaven?
2. According to Romans 3:23, how do we measure up to God's standard?
3. What is God's solution? (See 2 Corinthians 5:21.)
4. According to Ephesians 2:8-9, what role do good works play in our ability to get into heaven?
5. According to Ephesians 2:10, what role do good works play *after* we accept God's solution for our salvation?
6. Gandhi, who was famous for the good works he performed during his life, wrote, "The world's praise fails to move me, indeed it very often stings me." What do you think he meant?
7. What are *you* counting on to get into heaven?

QUESTION #8: ISN'T CHRISTIANITY JUST A PSYCHOLOGICAL CRUTCH?

1. What are some of the concrete evidences we have discussed in this book that indicate Christianity is an objective experience rather than a psychological one?
2. How would you answer a person who challenged your beliefs by claiming that you only accepted them because you were preconditioned by your upbringing?
3. Explain this comment from page 118: "The minds that reject (Christianity) are the minds that have not explored it honestly and fairly."

4. How is it correct to say that Christianity is a crutch?

5. What are some of the crutches that people who choose not to accept Christianity lean on?

6. How is Christianity *more* than just a crutch?

QUESTION #9: IS THERE REALLY A HELL? WHAT ABOUT HEAVEN?

1. What choice must a person make before God allows him or her to enter hell?

2. If you were God, what would you do with the people who died having rejected your free gift of salvation?

3. Explain how love as well as justice demands confinement of those who reject God.

4. Why can't God just ignore or annihilate those who reject Him?

5. Look up the following verses. How does Jesus describe hell?
   a. Matthew 5:22:
   b. Matthew 25:46:
   c. Mark 9:43-48:

6. What are you looking forward to most in heaven?

QUESTION #10: WHAT DOES IT MEAN TO BELIEVE?

1. How did God provide a bridge across the great chasm that separates sinful human beings from His perfect holiness?

2. What do each of the following Latin words for "believe" actually mean? Give an illustration for each:
   a. *noticia:*
   b. *assentia:*
   c. *fiducia:*

3. What does it actually mean to "believe in the Lord Jesus, and you will be saved" (Acts 16:31)?

4. According to the following verses, what are some of the joys that become ours when we believe and accept Jesus Christ's death on the cross as payment for our sins?

   a. John 3:16:

   b. John 1:12:

   c. Ephesians 1:3-10:

5. Have you accepted the gift of salvation that God is holding out to you? If so, tell when and how that happened.

QUESTION #11: CAN I BE SURE I'M GOING TO HEAVEN?

1. What is one thing that we know Jesus is doing in heaven right now (John 14:1-2)?

2. The Bible describes the time that it took Jesus to complete the creation of the whole world as "six days" (Genesis 1:31–2:2). He has already spent close to 2,000 years preparing a place for us in heaven. Describe how spectacular you think heaven will be. Do you think you will ever get bored?

3. If you have accepted God's gift of eternal life through Jesus' sacrifice, is there any way that you can lose that gift? Read Romans 8:38-39.

4. How does sin affect your relationship with God? How does it affect your fellowship with Him?

5. How does God's gift of "eternal" life make Christianity different from all other world religions?

6. How should knowing you have "eternal" life affect the way you live today?

7. How do you hope Jesus will decorate your room in heaven?

NOTES

QUESTION #1: CAN YOU PROVE TO ME THAT THERE IS A GOD?
1. Sharon Begley, "Science Finds God," *Newsweek*, July 20, 1998, pp. 46-49.

QUESTION #3: HOW DO WE KNOW THAT THE BIBLE IS A RELIABLE SOURCE?
1. Ken Boa and Larry Moody, *I'm Glad You Asked* (Wheaton, Ill.: Victor, 1994), p. 97.
2. Boa and Moody, pp. 97-98.
3. Josh McDowell, *A Ready Defense* (Nashville: Thomas Nelson, 1993), pp. 109-110.
4. Josh McDowell, *Evidence That Demands a Verdict* (Arrowhead Springs, Calif.: Campus Crusade for Christ, Inc., 1972), pp. 67, 84-85.
5. Boa and Moody, p. 95; McDowell, *A Ready Defense*, pp. 86-87.
6. Boa and Moody, pp. 106-107.
7. McDowell, *Evidence That Demands a Verdict*, p. 48.
8. Boa and Moody, p. 92.
9. Paul Little, *Know What You Believe* (Wheaton, Ill.: Victor, 1970), p. 20.
10. Lois M. Gurel, "Pin," *The World Book Encyclopedia*, vol. 15 (Chicago: World Book, Inc., 1998), p. 466.

QUESTION #4: DID THE MIRACLES IN THE BIBLE REALLY HAPPEN?
1. David DeWitt, *Beyond the Basics: Answering Questions Christians Ask* (Chicago: Moody, 1983), p. 78.
2. Edwin A. Abbott, *Flatland* (New York: Penguin, 1998), p. 86.
3. Charles W. Colson, *Loving God* (Grand Rapids, Mich.: Zondervan, 1987), p. 67.
4. Colson, pp. 68-69.

5. Josh McDowell, *Evidence That Demands a Verdict* (Arrowhead Springs, Calif.: Campus Crusade for Christ, Inc., 1972), p. 201.

6. C. S. Lewis, *Surprised by Joy: The Shape of My Early Life* (San Diego: Harcourt Brace, 1955), p. 229.

QUESTION #5: ISN'T IT NARROW-MINDED TO SAY THAT JESUS IS THE ONLY WAY TO GOD?

1. C. S. Lewis, *Mere Christianity* (New York: Macmillan, 1952), pp. 55-56.

2. Paul Little, *Know Why You Believe* (Wheaton, Ill.: Victor, 1967), p. 132.

QUESTION #6: WHAT ABOUT THOSE WHO HAVE NEVER HEARD ABOUT JESUS?

1. Richard Tkachuck, "Panspermia," *Origins*, 1983, vol. 10, no. 2, March 14, 1999.

2. Mohandas K. Gandhi, *The Story of My Experiment with Truth* (Boston: Beacon Press, 1957), xv.

QUESTION #7: ISN'T LIVING A GOOD LIFE GOOD ENOUGH?

1. Paul Little, *Know Why You Believe* (Wheaton, Ill.: Victor, 1967), p. 133.

2. Mohandas K. Gandhi, *The Story of My Experiment with Truth* (Boston: Beacon Press, 1957), pp. 504-505.

3. Ken Boa and Larry Moody, *I'm Glad You Asked* (Wheaton, Ill.: Victor, 1994), p. 227.

QUESTION #8: ISN'T CHRISTIANITY JUST A PSYCHOLOGICAL CRUTCH?

1. Guenter Lewy, *Why America Needs Religion* (Grand Rapids, Mich.: Eerdmans, 1996), x.

2. Lewy, pp. 112, 125.

QUESTION #9: IS THERE REALLY A HELL? WHAT ABOUT HEAVEN?

1. John J. Gerstner, "The Bible and Hell," *His*, January 1968.

2. Peter Kreeft, *Your Questions, God's Answers* (San Francisco: Ignatius, 1994), p. 119.

QUESTION #10: WHAT DOES IT MEAN TO BELIEVE?
1. David DeWitt, *Answering the Tough Ones* (Grand Rapids, Mich.: Relational Concepts, 1993), p. 108.

QUESTION #11: CAN I BE SURE I'M GOING TO HEAVEN?
1. James Strong, *Greek Dictionary of the New Testament* (Nashville: Royal, 1979), p. 9.

ABOUT THE AUTHOR

GWENDOLYN MITCHELL DIAZ BEGAN LIFE AS A MISSIONARY KID IN Nigeria, but moved to the United States at age ten. A graduate of the University of Pennsylvania, she spent many years working in the medical profession and writing articles and columns about sports, family, and her faith in God. She also has published the books *The Adventures of Mighty Mom* and *Mighty Mom's Secrets for Raising Super Kids.*

As a mother of four boys, Gwen feels particularly passionate about helping teens solidify their faith and grow as Christians. *Sticking Up for What I Believe* emerges from her many years as a parent. Gwen, along with her husband Ed, wanted to explain Christianity to teens in a way that "captured their interest, satisfied their curiosity, and communicated God's exciting truths to them."

INTERACTIVE GUIDES FOR FEEDING YOUR FAITH.

How to Stay Christian in College

Going away to college can mean students leave behind their network of support. This interactive guide helps them know what to expect, gives them tools to use, and reassures them they can grow in their faith at school.

(J. Budziszewski)

Walk This Way

In a fun format that is easy to use, this book presents the Beatitudes as the "eight steps" to becoming Jesus' disciple.

(Tim Woodroof)

To get your copies, visit your local bookstore, call 1-800-366-7788, or log on to www.navpress.com. Ask for a FREE catalog of NavPress products. Offer #BPA.

NAVPRESS

BRINGING TRUTH TO LIFE
www.navpress.com